Buddhism and Tourism:
An Indian Experience

BUDDHISM AND TOURISM

An Indian Experience

Dr. Kranti P. Sawarkar
Subodh Kumar Mishra

KANISHKA PUBLISHERS, DISTRIBUTORS
NEW DELHI-110 002

KANISHKA PUBLISHERS, DISTRIBUTORS
4697/5-21 A, Ansari Road, Daryaganj
New Delhi-110 002
Phones : 2327 0497, 2328 8285
Fax : 011-2328 8285
E-mail: kanishka_publishing@yahoo.co.in

Buddhism and Tourism: An Indian Experience

First Published 2009

ISBN 978-81-8457-162-2

PRINTED IN INDIA

Published by Madan Sachdeva for Kanishka Publishers, Distributors, 4697/5-21A, Ansari Road, Daryaganj, New Delhi-110 002, Typeset by Sunshine Graphics, Delhi, and Printed at Rajdhani Printers, Delhi.

Preface

Buddhism which often referred as a religion is actually a set of teachings about the way of life. These set of teachings were made popular by Siddhartha Gautama popularly known as Lord Gautama Buddha, some 2500 years ago. Today Buddhism is practiced more in other countries than India–its birthplace. It is surprising and interesting to note that the some of the most developed economies of the world–China, Japan, Korea–all are guided by principles of Buddhism.

At the dawn of independence, architects of Indian republic were fascinated by Buddhist philosophy and it reflects in the national insignia in more than one form:

(a) The seal of Indian Government–The Lion Pillar–is taken from the pillar erected at the place where Lord Buddha gave her first preaching–Sarnath.

(b) The wheel in the middle of our national flag is named after King Ashoka who is well known for popularizing Buddhism off-shore.

(c) The principle of socialism mentioned in the preamble of our constitution is based on Buddhist philosophy "Bhavatu sabba mangalam" (May all being be happy!).

(d) Many of the fundamental rights and directive principles of state policy enshrined in the constitution are deeply rooted in the Buddhist principle of well being of animals, plants and humans alike.

(e) Today non-violence is touted as Gandhian philosophy. In fact, Gandhiji was so moved by the Buddhist philosophy of non-violence and communal harmony that he made it his way of life.

Even modern India's foreign policy–Panchsheel–is of Buddhist origin!

All these really prompt us to ask ourselves questions like who discovered Buddhism? What prompted him to do so? How did he do it? How did Buddhism migrate from India to other countries?

The following Chapters attempt to answer the above. It also enlists the places associated with Buddhism. In case one is interested to visit them, it gives a readymade solution in the form of Mahaparinirvan Express–a special train touching the prominent Buddhist places.

Come……Let's walk in the footstep of Lord Buddha…….

BHAVATU SABBA MANGALAM !!!
(May all beings be happy !!!)

Dr. Kranti P. Sawarkar
Subodh Kumar Mishra

Contents

1
A Brief Biography

Birth of Lord Buddha

Though the exact date is uncertain Lord Buddha is said to be born to King Suddhodana and her queen Maya in Kapilavastu, Lumbini, which is in present-day Nepal between 400 and 480 BC.

King Suddhodana led the Shakya clansmen who dwelt along the river Rohini that flowed among the southern foothills of the Himalayas. He had transferred his capital to Kapila and there had built a great castle and had ruled wisely, winning the joyful acclaim of his people. Queen Maya was the daughter of the King's uncle who was also a king of the neighbouring division of the same Shakya clan. For twenty years they had no children.

Different stories surround the conception and actual birth of the Buddha. One has it that around the time of the Buddha's conception, Mahamaya had a dream in which she saw a large white elephant enter her side. This was interpreted by the Brahmins, or priests of the day, that the child would grow up to be a great emperor or a great holyman, the elephant being an auspicious symbol of sovereignty. The King and the people looked forward with joyful expectancy to the birth of a royal child. According to their custom the Queen returned to her own home for the birth, and while on the way, in the beautiful spring sunshine, she rested in the flower garden of Lumbini Park. All about her were Asoka blossoms and in delight she reached out her right arm to pluck a branch and the Prince was born.

Another tells how Mahamaya, on her way to visiting her relatives, gave birth to the Buddha standing up and holding on to a tree, which is why the Buddha seems to have been born at Lumbini rather than his father's town of Kapilavasthu.

According to legend, as soon as he was born, the Buddha walked seven steps and announced: 'I am the highest in the world; I am the best in the world; I am the foremost in the world. This is my last birth; now there is no renewal of being for me'.

The joy of the King was extreme as he named the child: Siddhartha, which means, "Every wish fulfilled." All expressed their heartfelt delight and extolled the glory of the Queen and her princely child; even Heaven and Earth manifested their joy. This was a full moon day – "Baishakh Purnima". In the palace of the King, however, delight was quickly followed by sorrow, for after a few days lovely Queen Maya suddenly passed away. Fortunately her younger sister, Prajapati became the child's foster mother and brought him up with loving care.

A hermit, who lived in the mountains not far away, noticing a glory about the castle and interpreting it as a good omen, came down to the palace and was shown the child. He predicted: "This prince, if he remains in the palace after his youth, will become a great King to rule the Four Seas. But if he forsakes the household life to embrace a religious life, he will become a Buddha and the world's Savior." At first the King was pleased because of the prophecy, but later became troubled at the thought of the possibility of his only son leaving the palace to become a homeless recluse.

Childhood and Marriage

At the age of seven the Prince began his lessons in literature and the military arts, but his thoughts more naturally ran to other things. One spring day he went out of the castle with his father and they were watching a farmer at his plowing; he noticed a bird flying down to the ground and carrying away a little worm which had been thrown out of the ground by the farmer's plough. He, who had lost his mother so soon after his birth, was deeply affected by the tragedy of these two little creatures. He sat down in the shade of a tree and thought about it, whispering to himself:

"Alas! Do all living creatures kill each other?"

This spiritual wound was deepened day after day as he grew up; like a little scar on a young tree, the sufferings of human life were more and more deeply carved into his mind.

A Life of Pleasure

There seems no doubt that the Buddha was born into a wealthy and privileged family and that materially he wanted for nothing. In the *Magandiya Sutra* the Buddha describes his home life: 'I enjoyed myself...I had three palaces, one for the rainy season, one for the winter, and one for the summer. I lived in the rains' palace for the four months of the rainy season, enjoying myself with musicians who were all female'.

The King was increasingly worried as he recalled the hermit's prophecy and tried in every possible way to cheer the Prince and to turn his thoughts in other directions. At the age of sixteen, the King arranged the marriage of the Prince to the Princess Yasodhara, who was the daughter of Suprabuddha, Lord of Koliya castle and a brother of the late Queen Maya.

For ten years the Prince was immersed in a round of music, dancing and pleasure, in the different pavilions of spring, autumn and winter, but ever his thoughts reverted to the problem of suffering as he pensively tried to understand the true meaning of human life.

The Four Sights

Because of the prophecies that attended Siddhartha's birth–that he would either become a world ruler or a great holyman–his father, Suddhodhana tried to shield his son from the more distressing features of the world. Consequently, Siddhartha spent his life with the confines of the palace and its grounds, absorbed in pleasure.

But dissatisfaction grew to the extent that one day Siddhartha asked his charioteer to take him on an excursion outside of the place. On the first visit he encountered an old man. On the next excursion he encountered a sick man. On his third excursion, he encountered a corpse being carried to cremation. Such sights brought home to him the prevalence of suffering in the world and that he too was subject to old age, sickness and death—that no-one, not even a king's son, could escape these three. What hope was there, what point in living, if this was the destiny of all? On his fourth excursion, however, he encountered a holyman or *sadhu*, apparently content and at peace with the world. Perhaps, there *was* a way out of what seemed like the inevitability of suffering after all! (In Buddhism these are referred to as 'the four sights' or 'four signs'.)

Shortly after this, however—at the age of twenty-nine-Siddhartha's life took a radical change in direction...

The Struggle Within

At what point the Buddha's disaffection for his life of luxury began to manifest itself is hard to determine. It is likely that it was something that he struggled with for a long time before, at the age of twenty-nine, he decided to leave the palace, his life of pleasure and comfort, and even his wife, Yasodhara, and child, Rahula. The factors that must have led up this emphatic and irrevocable decision have been crystallized in the traditional account.

Luxuries of the palace, healthy bodies, rejoicing youth! What do they mean to me?" he meditated. "Some day we may be sick, we shall become aged, from death we can not eventually escape. Pride of youth, pride of health, pride of existence, all thoughtful people must cast them aside."

"A man struggling for existence will naturally look for help. There are two ways of looking for help, a right way and a wrong way. To look the wrong way means that, while he recognizes that sickness, old age and death are unavoidable, he looks for help among the same class of empty, transitory things. To look the right way means that he recognizes the true nature of sickness, old age and death, and looks for life in that which transcends all human suffering. In this palace life of pleasure I seem to be looking for help in the wrong way."

The Leaving

Thus the mental struggle went on in the mind of the Prince until his twenty-ninth year when his only child, Rahula, was born. This seemed to bring things to a climax and he decided to leave his palace home and seek the solution of his mental unrest in the homeless life of a mendicant. This plan he carried out one night, by leaving the castle with only his personal servant, Channa, and his favourite horse, the snow-white Kanthaka, and even these he left behind him when he had crossed the river at the bounds of his Father's kingdom.

It was not easy for Siddhartha to leave his home and family. As his wife and child lay sleeping, he said his goodbyes, fearing that if his wife should wake he wouldn't be able to leave. And then he was gone, to begin life as a wandering holyman in search of the ultimate...

But his mental troubles were not at an end and many doubts beset him. "Perhaps it would be better for me to return to the castle and seek some other solution; then the whole world will be mine." But he resisted these doubts by realizing that nothing worldly could satisfy him. So he shaved his head, carried a begging bowl in his hand, and turned his mendicant steps to the south.

The Quest Begins

After leaving his father's palace and his family, Siddhartha embarked upon the life of a wanderer, sleeping in forests and living off the food given to him by those he came into contact with. At first he sought out those who might teach him how to progress further along his spiritual path, teachers such as Alara Kalama and Uddaka Ramaputta. Through the meditation techniques taught by them, he was able to reach higher states of knowledge, but fell short of complete enlightenment. Though he became a teacher under Ramaputta, he came to realize that what he had learnt so far did not 'lead to disenchantment, to dispassion, to cessation, to peace, to enlightenment, to *Nibbana*'.

Finally he went to the Magadha country and practiced asceticism in the forest of Uruvilva on the banks of the Nairanjana river where it flows by the Gaya Castle.

The methods of his practice were unbelievably intense. He spurred himself on with the thought that "no ascetic in the past, none in the present, and none in the future, ever have or ever will practice more earnestly that I do."

Still, the Prince could not get what he sought. After six years in the forest he gave up the practice of asceticism. He bathed in the river and accepted a bowl of food from the hand of Sujata, a maid who lived in the neighbouring village. The five companions who had lived with the Prince for the six years of his ascetic practices looked on with amazement that he could receive food from the hand of a maiden; they thought him degraded thereby and left him. The Prince, thus, was left alone. He was still feeble but at the risk of his life he attempted a final meditation, saying to himself, "Blood may become exhausted, flesh may decay, bones may fall apart, but I will never leave this place until I find the way to enlightenment."

Enlightenment

MAHABODHI TREE

Siddhartha then made his way to a place near Bodh Gaya in India, where he found a suitable site for meditation. There he remained, emphasizing a meditation called "space-like concentration on the Dharmakaya" in which he focused single-pointedly on the ultimate nature of all phenomena. After training in this meditation for six years he realized that he was very close to attaining full enlightenment, and so he walked to Bodh Gaya where, on the full moon day of the fourth month of the lunar calendar, he seated himself beneath the Bodhi Tree in the meditation posture and vowed not to rise from meditation until he had attained perfect enlightenment. With this determination he entered the space-like concentration on the Dharmakaya.

It was an intense and incomparable struggle! His mind was desperate, was filled with confusing thoughts, dark shadows overhung his spirit, he was beset with all the lures of evil. But carefully and patiently he examined them one by one and rejected them all. It, indeed, was a hard struggle, that made his blood run thin, his flesh creep, and his bones crack. But when the morning star appeared in the eastern sky, the struggle was over and the Prince's mind was as clear and bright as the day-break. He had found the path to enlightenment at last. It was About 528 BC, when he was thirty-five years of age that the Prince became Buddha.

The First Teaching

From this time on the Prince was known by different names; some spoke of him as Buddha, the Perfectly Enlightened One; some spoke of him as Shakyamuni, the Sage of the Shakya clan; and still others spoke of him affectionately as the Blessed One. He went first to Mrigadava in Varanasi where the five mendicants who had lived with him during the six years of his ascetic life were staying. At first they shunned him, but after he had talked with them, they believed in him and became his first followers. It was to these five in the Deer Park at Sarnath near Varanasi that the Buddha Gave his first teaching, referred to as 'Setting into Motion the Wheel of Dhamma'.

In his first sermon, the Buddha advises against the two extremes of luxury and self-mortification and offers a 'Middle Way'. This Middle Way is to be understood in the context of the Four Noble Truths, the distillation of the Buddha's message. These are 'the noble truth of suffering...the noble truth of the origin of suffering...the noble truth of the cessation of suffering...the noble truth leading the way to the cessation of suffering'. The last of these, the Eightfold Path is the Buddha's teaching on what must be done to achieve enlightenment. It consists of eight factors that incorporate wisdom, morality and concentration. The eight factors are:

Right Understanding,

Right Thought,

Right Speech,

Right Action,

Right Livelihood,

Right Effort,

Right Mindfulness, and

Right Concentration.

The Dissemination

The Buddha spent the rest of his life as a homeless, itinerant teacher. His life and needs were simple. For nine months of the year he travelled on foot, offering his teachings to any that were interested. He went from village to village, and from town to town, using his alms bowl as a means of obtaining sustenance. In this way he came into contact with all levels of society, relating the same message to all those he encountered: life is suffering, craving is the cause of this suffering, there is an end to suffering, and there is a means to bring this suffering to an end.

Wherever he went, Buddha touched the life of the people. This was evident from many anecdotes of his time. Some of them are represented below.

Kisa Gotami was grief stricken when her only son died when still a baby. She refused to believe he was truly dead. Eventually she met the Buddha who said he could help her but she must get a handful of mustard seed from a house where there had been no death. She went from house to house but everywhere she met people who shared their own grief of lost friends and relatives. Kisa Gotami realised her stupidity and had her son cremated. She became a nun and eventually realised enlightenment.

Patachara came from a wealthy family but ran away with one of the servants. Several years later she has two children and wants to see her family and get their forgiveness. She sets out but her husband and the two children are killed. She finally arrives home only to find that her parents are also dead. She ordains as a nun and became enlightened when washing her feet. She noticed that the water ran across the ground a little and soaked in, on pouring a little more she noticed it ran a little further, and a third time. Her insight was that some die young, some in middle age, some old age - but all must die.

Angulimala had already collected 999 fingers and needed just one more to make up the 1,000 that he was seeking. He would not have hesitated in killing his own mother to reach his goal, but to do so would have put him in danger of going to the worst hell. To kill either of one's parents is one of the worst sins that one can perform.

The Buddha, with his psychic powers, was able to see what Angulimala was about to do and, out of his great compassion, decided to try to prevent this horrible crime. As the Buddha approached the forest, village people warned him not to enter, as Angulimala was very strong and was sure to kill anybody, including monks. The Buddha continued on the path in silence. At first Angulimala saw his mother approaching. So steeped was his mind in killing that he didn't mind killing his mother to gain the final finger.

As he descended on the path, suddenly the Buddha appeared between him and his mother. He thought, "Why should I kill my mother for the sake of one finger when there is someone else? Let her live."

He didn't realize that it was also a very serious offense to kill a monk, but he could only think of the one finger needed to complete his necklace. The Angulimala sutra says: "Now Angulimala took his sword and shield and buckled on his bow and quiver and he followed behind the Blessed One. Then the Blessed One performed such a feat of supernormal power that the bandit Angulimala, going as fast as he could, was unable to catch up with the Blessed One who was walking at his normal pace."

Angulimala was amazed that no matter how fast he was travelling, he was unable to catch up with the Buddha. He called,

"Stop, monk! Stop, monk!" The Buddha replied, "I have stopped, Angulimala. You should stop too."

Angulimala thought, "These monks are supposed to tell the truth, but this monk continues to walk when he tells me he has stopped. I must ask him what he means when he says that he has stopped."

The Buddha explained to him, "Angulimala, I have stopped forever, giving up violence to every living being, but you have no restraint toward things that breathe. That is why I have stopped and you have not."

When Angulimala heard these words, a great change came over him. He felt deeply moved by the wise words of the Buddha. He said, "I will for sure renounce all evil after hearing this dharma." He threw his sword and weapons over a cliff and bowed at the Buddha's feet.

He asked the Buddha if he could become his disciple as a monk. The Buddha replied, "Come, Bhikkhu." And that is how he became a monk.

The Sangha

As he travelled, he gathered a following of those who wanted to take up the same life of simplicity in the hope of gaining enlightenment. Such followers came from all strata of society, rich and poor. The only requirement was a sincere desire to follow the Buddha's teaching. The commitment had to be total. It meant leaving one's family - just as the Buddha himself had done - and leading a life of celibacy and strict morality. It also meant having few possessions and maintaining a simple lifestyle. Gradually, the number of followers increased and eventually a definite community of monks, and later nuns, was formed known as the Sangha.

For forty-five years, the Buddha continued to spread his teachings, urging his monks to 'Go forth...for the benefit of many, for the happiness of many, out of compassion for the world. Preach to them the, which is Dhamma, beautiful in the beginning, beautiful in the middle, and beautiful at the end...'.

The Parinibbana

The Buddha's teaching spanned forty-five years and, at the age of eighty, his unique journey came to an end. The actual cause of death was said to be food-poisoning but three months before his passing away, the Buddha had indicated that he would soon die. Despite being unwell in the months leading up to his death, the Buddha continued to travel and teach, finally coming to a small village called Kushinagar, in today's Uttar Pradesh.

Mahaparinirvana

For forty-five years the Buddha went about the country preaching and persuading men to follow his way of life, but at last, at Vaisali on the way from Rajagriha to Sravasti, he became ill and predicted that after three months he would enter Nirvana. Still he journeyed on until he reached Pava where he was made critically ill by food offered by Cunda, a blacksmith.

Then by easy stages in spite of great pain and weakness, he reached the forest on the border of Kuninagara castle. Lying between two large sala trees, he continued his teachings to his favourite disciples until the last moment. Thus passed into the unknown the greatest of the world's teachers and the kindest of men.

Final Words

As monks and lay people gathered round, Ananda, the Buddha's long time and most devoted attendant broke down in tears as he realized that his Lord was about to die. But the Buddha told him not to weep and wail, saying, 'Have I not already told you that all things that are pleasurable and delightful are changeable, subject to separation...?...Ananda, make the effort, and in a short time you will be free of the corruptions'. He too, the Buddha, was subject to impermanence, just like anything else in *samsara.*

One of the concerns of his followers was what would become of the Sangha after he died. Who would lead them? The Buddha said: '"Ananda, it may be that you will think: 'The Teacher's instruction has ceased, now we have no teacher!' It should not be seen like this, Ananda, for what I have taught and explained to you as *Dhamma* and discipline will, at my passing, be your teacher."'

The Buddha's final words were, as ever, pragmatic and encouraging: 'All things are impermanent - strive on with diligence!'

As he lay dying, the Buddha entered into each of the meditative states known as *jhanas*, before passing away into *nibbana* completely. This is referred to as the Buddha's *parinibbana.* No longer would he be reborn, he had entered the deathless state never to return.

Relics

After had died many of the monks fell into great lamentation, only to be reprimanded by one of their seniors, the Venerable Anuruddha: 'Friends, enough of your weeping and wailing! Has not the Lord already told you that all things that are pleasant and delightful are changeable...? So why all this, friend? Whatever is born, become, compounded is subject to decay'. The body of the Buddha was kept for seven days so that his followers could pay their last respects and then under the oversight of Ananda, the Buddha's favorite disciple, the body was cremated by his friends in Kusinagara castle. Seven of the neighbouring rulers under the lead of King Ajatasatru demanded that the ashes be divided among them. The King of the Kunsinagara castle at first refused and the dispute even threatened to end in war, but by the advice of a wise man named Dona, the crises passed and the ashes were divided and buried under eight great monuments. Even the embers of the fire and the earthen jar that had held the ashes were divided and given to two others to be likewise honoured. His relics were shared out amongst his followed and enshrined in *stupas*.

The importance of the Buddha lies in the fact that he was unique human being who, through his own efforts, discovered a means of ending the cycle of suffering inherent in *samsara*. More importantly, he was willing to share what he had discovered with the world at large. His legacy is his teachings which have as profound a significance now as they did over 2500 years ago.

2

Buddhism After Lord Buddha's *Mahaparinirvan*

Early Buddhism

Before the royal sponsorship of Ashoka the Great in the 3rd century BCE, Buddhism seems to have remained a relatively minor phenomenon, and the historicity of its formative events is poorly established. Two formative councils are supposed to have taken place, although our knowledge of them is based on much later accounts. The councils tend to explain the formalization of the Buddhist doctrine, and the various subsequent schisms inside the Buddhist movement.

1st Buddhist Council (5th c. BCE)

The first Buddhist council was held soon after the death of the Buddha under the patronage of king Ajatasatru of the Magadha Empire, and presided by a monk named Mahakasyapa, at Rajagriha (today's Rajgir). The objective of the council was to record the Buddha's sayings (sutra) and codify monastic rules (vinaya): Ananda, one of the Buddha's main disciples and his cousin, was called upon to recite the discourses of the Buddha, and Upali, another disciple, recited the rules of the vinaya. These became the basis of the Pali Canon, which has been the orthodox text of reference throughout the history of Buddhism.

2nd Buddhist Council (383 BCE)

The second Buddhist council was convened by King Kalasoka and held at Vaisali, following conflicts between the traditional schools of Buddhism and a more liberal interpretational movement called the Mahasanghikas. The traditional schools considered the Buddha as a human being who reached enlightenment, which could be most easily attained by monks following the monastic rules and practicing the teaching for the sake of overcoming suffering and attaining Arahantship. The secessionist Mahasangikas, however, tended to consider this approach too individualistic and selfish. They considered the objective of becoming an arhat insufficient, and instead proposed that the only true goal was to reach full Buddhahood, in a sense opening the way to future Mahāyāna thought. They became proponents of more relaxed monastic rules, which could appeal to a large majority of monastic and lay people (hence their name the "great" or "majority" assembly).

The council ended with the rejection of the Mahasanghikas. They left the council and maintained themselves for several centuries in northwestern India and Central Asia according to Kharoshti inscriptions found near the Oxus and dated c. 1st century CE.

Ashokan Era

The Mauryan Emperor Ashoka the Great (273–232 BCE) converted to Buddhism after his bloody conquest of the territory of Kalinga (modern Orissa) in eastern India during the Kalinga War. Regretful of the horrors brought by the conflict, the king decided to renounce violence, and propagate the faith by building stupas and pillars urging for the respect of all animal life, and enjoining people to follow the Dharma. Perhaps the finest example of these is the Great Stupa in Sanchi, India (near Bhopal). It was constructed in the third century BCE and later enlarged. Its carved gates, called Tohans, are considered among the finest examples of Buddhist art in India. He also built roads, hospitals, resthouses, universities and irrigation systems around the country. He treated his subjects as equals regardless of their religion, politics or caste.

This period marks the first spread of Buddhism beyond India. According to the plates and pillars left by Ashoka (the Edicts of Ashoka), emissaries were sent to various countries in order to spread Buddhism, as far as the Greek kingdoms in the West, in particular the neighbouring Greco-Bactrian Kingdom, and possibly even farther to the Mediterranean.

3rd Buddhist Council (c. 250 BCE)

King Ashoka convened the third Buddhist council around 250 BCE at Pataliputra (today's Patna). It was held by the monk Moggaliputta. The objective of the council was to reconcile the different schools of Buddhism, to purify the Buddhist movement, particularly from opportunistic factions which had been attracted by the royal patronage, and to organize the dispatch of Buddhist missionaries throughout the known world.

The Pali canon (Tipitaka, or Tripitaka in Sanskrit, literally the "Three Baskets"), which comprises the texts of reference of traditional Buddhism and is considered to be directly transmitted from the Buddha, was formalized at that time. It consists of the doctrine (the Sutra Pitaka), the monastic discipline (Vinaya Pitaka) and an additional new body of subtle philosophy (the Abhidharma Pitaka).

The efforts of Ashoka to purify the Buddhist faith also had the effect of segregating against other emerging movements. In particular, after 250 BCE, the Sarvastivadin (who had been rejected by the 3rd council, according to the Theravada tradition) and the Dharmaguptaka schools became quite influential in northwestern India and Central Asia, up to the time of the Kushan Empire in the first centuries of the common era. The Dharmaguptakas were characterized by a belief that Buddha was separate, and above, the rest of the Buddhist community. The Sarvastivadin believed that past, present, and future are all simultaneous.

Buddhism in Hellenistic World

Some of the Edicts of Ashoka inscriptions describe the efforts made by Ashoka to propagate the Buddhist faith throughout the Hellenistic world, which at that time formed an uninterrupted continuum from the borders of India to Greece. The Edicts indicate a clear understanding of the political organization in Hellenistic territories: the names and location of the main Greek monarchs of the time are identified, and they are claimed as recipients of Buddhist proselytism: Antiochus II Theos of the Seleucid Kingdom (261–246 BCE), Ptolemy II Philadelphos of Egypt (285–247 BCE), Antigonus Gonatas of Macedonia (276–239 BCE), Magas of Cyrene (288–258 BCE) in Cyrenaica (modern Libya), and Alexander II of Epirus (272–255 BCE) in Epirus (modern Albania).

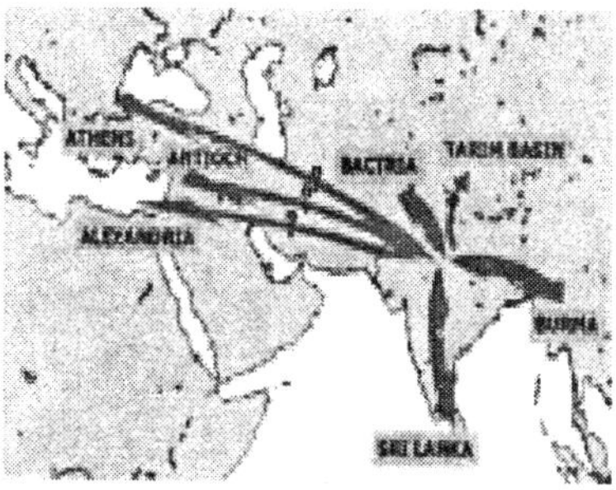

Buddhist proselytism at the time of king Ashoka (260–218 BCE), according to the Edicts of Ashoka.

"The conquest by Dharma has been won here, on the borders, and even six hundred yojanas (5,400–9,600 km) away, where the Greek king Antiochos rules, beyond there where the four kings named Ptolemy, Antigonos, Magas and Alexander rule, likewise in the south among the Cholas, the Pandyas, and as far as Tamraparni (Sri Lanka)." (Edicts of Ashoka, 13th Rock Edict, S. Dhammika). Furthermore, according to Pali sources, some of Ashoka's emissaries were Greek Buddhist monks, indicating close religious exchanges between the two cultures: "When the thera (elder) Moggaliputta, the illuminator of the religion of the Conqueror (Ashoka), had brought the (third) council to an end (...) he sent forth theras, one here and one there: (...) and to Aparantaka (the "Western countries" corresponding to Gujarat and Sindh) he sent the Greek (Yona) named Dhammarakkhita". (Mahavamsa XII).

Ashoka also issued Edicts in the Greek language as well as in Aramaic. One of them, found in Kandahar, advocates the adoption of "Piety" (using the Greek term Eusebeia for Dharma) to the Greek community:

"Ten years (of reign) having been completed, King Piodasses (Ashoka) made known (the doctrine of) Piety to men; and from this moment he has made men more pious, and everything thrives throughout the whole world."

It is not clear how much these interactions may have been influential, but some authors have commented that some level of syncretism between Hellenist thought and Buddhism may have started in Hellenic lands at that time. They have pointed to the presence of Buddhist communities in the Hellenistic world around that period, in particular in Alexandria (mentioned by Clement of Alexandria), and to the pre-Christian monastic order of the Therapeutae (possibly a deformation of the Pali word "Theravada"), who may have "almost entirely drawn (its) inspiration from the teaching and practices of Buddhist asceticism", and may even have been descendants of Ashoka's emissaries to the West. The philosopher Hegesias of Cyrene, from the city of Cyrene where Magas of Cyrene ruled, is sometimes thought to have been influenced by the teachings of Ashoka's Buddhist missionaries.

Buddhist gravestones from the Ptolemaic period have also been found in Alexandria, decorated with depictions of the Dharma wheel (Tarn, "The Greeks in Bactria and India"). Commenting on the presence of Buddhists in Alexandria, some scholars have even pointed out that "It was later in this very place that some of the most active centers of Christianity were established" (Robert Linssen "Zen living").

In the 2nd century CE, the Christian dogmatist Clement of Alexandria recognized Bactrian Buddhists (Sramanas) and Indian Gymnosophists for their influence on Greek thought:

"Thus philosophy, a thing of the highest utility, flourished in antiquity among the barbarians, shedding its light over the nations. And afterwards it came to Greece. First in its ranks were the prophets of the Egyptians; and the Chaldeans among the Assyrians; and the Druids among the Gauls; and the *Sramanas* among the Bactrians and the philosophers of the Celts; and the Magi of the Persians, who foretold the Saviour's birth, and came into the land of Judaea guided by a star. The Indian gymnosophists are also in the number, and the other barbarian philosophers. And of these there are two classes, some of them called *Sramanas*, and others Brahmins Clement of Alexandria "The Stromata, or Miscellanies" Book I, Chapter XV.

Early Asian Expansion

Sri Lanka was allegedly proselytized by Ashoka's son Mahinda and six companions during the 2nd century BCE. They converted the king Devanampiya Tissa and many of the nobility. This is when the Mahavihara monastery, a center of Sinhalese orthodoxy, was built. The Pali Canon was put in writing in Sri Lanka during the reign of king Vittagamani (29–17 BCE), and the Theravada tradition flourished there, harboring some great commentators such as Buddhaghosa (4th–5th century). Although Mahayana Buddhism gained some influence at that time, Theravada ultimately prevailed, and Sri Lanka turned out to be the last stronghold of Theravada Buddhism, from where it would expand again to South-East Asia from the 11th century. In the areas east of the Indian subcontinent (modern Burma and Thailand), Indian culture strongly influenced the Mons. The Mons are said to have been converted to Buddhism from the 3rd century BCE under the proselytizing of the Indian Emperor Ashoka the Great, before the fission between Mahayana and Hinayana Buddhism. Early Mon Buddhist temples, such as Peikthano in central Burma, have been dated between the 1st and the 5th century CE.

The Buddhist art of the Mons was especially influenced by the Indian art of the Gupta and post-Gupta periods, and their mannerist style spread widely in South-East Asia following the expansion of the Mon kingdom between the 5th and 8th centuries. The Theravada faith expanded in the northern parts of Southeast Asia under Mon influence, until it was progressively displaced by Mahayana Buddhism from around the 6th century CE. According to the *Ashokavadana* (2nd century CE), Ashoka sent a missionary to the north, through the Himalayas, to Khotan in the Tarim Basin, then the land of the Tocharians, speakers of an Indo-European language.

Rise of the Sunga (2nd–1st c. BCE)

The Sunga dynasty (185–73 BCE) was established in 185 BCE, about 50 years after Ashoka's death. After assassinating King Brhadrata (last of the Mauryan rulers), military commander-in-chief Pusyamitra Sunga took the throne. Buddhist religious scriptures such as the Ashokavadana allege that Pusyamitra (an orthodox Brahmin) was hostile towards Buddhists and persecuted the Buddhist faith. Buddhists wrote that he "destroyed monasteries and killed Monks" : 84,000 Buddhist stupas which had been built by Ashoka were "destroyed" (R. Thaper), and 100 gold coins were offered for the head of each Buddhist monk . In addition, Buddhist sources allege that a large number of Buddhist monasteries (viharas) were converted to Hindu temples, in such places as Nalanda, Bodhgaya, Sarnath, or Mathura.

Following Ashoka's sponsorship of Buddhism, it is possible that Buddhist institutions fell on harder times under the Sungas but no evidence of active persecution has been noted. Etienne Lamotte observes: *"To judge from the documents, Pushyamitra must be acquitted through lack of proof."* Another eminent historian, Romila Thapar, points to archaeological evidence that "suggests the contrary [to the claim that Pusyamitra was a fanatical anti-Buddhist]" and never actually destroyed 84000 stupas as claimed by Buddhist works. Thapar stresses that Buddhist accounts are probably hyperbolic renditions of Pusyamitra's attack of the Mauryas, and merely reflect the frustration of the Buddhist religious figures to the decline in the importance of their religion by the Sungas.

During the period, Buddhist monks deserted the Ganges valley, following either the Northern road (Uttarapatha) or the Southern road (Daksinapatha). Conversely, Buddhist artistic creation stopped in the old Magadha area, to reposition itself either in Northwest area of Gandhara and Mathura, or in the Southeast around Amaravati. Some artistic activity also occurred in central India, as in Bharhut, to which the Sungas may or may not have contributed.

Greco-Buddhist Interaction (2nd c. BCE–1st c. CE)

In the areas west of the Indian subcontinent, neighbouring Greek kingdoms had been in place in Bactria (today's northern Afghanistan) since the time of the conquests of Alexander the Great around 326 BCE: first the Seleucids from around 323 BCE, then the Greco-Bactrian kingdom from around 250 BCE. The Greco-Bactrian king Demetrius I invaded India in 180 BCE as far as Pataliputra, establishing an Indo-Greek kingdom that was to last in various part of northern India until the end of the 1st century BCE. Buddhism flourished under the Indo-Greek kings, and it has been suggested that their invasion of India was intended to show their support for the Mauryan empire, and to protect the Buddhist faith from the alleged religious persecutions of the Sungas (185–73 BCE). One of the most famous Indo-Greek kings is Menander (reigned c. 160–135 BCE). He apparently converted to Buddhism and is presented in the Mahayana tradition as one of the great benefactors of the faith, on a par with king Ashoka or the later Kushan king Kanishka. Menander's coins bear the mention "Saviour king" in Greek, and sometimes designs of the eight-spoked wheel. Direct cultural exchange is also suggested by the dialogue of the Milinda Panha between Menander and the monk Nagasena around 160 BCE. Upon his death, the honour of sharing his remains was claimed by the cities under his rule, and they were enshrined in stupas, in a parallel with the historic Buddha (Plutarch, Praec. reip. ger. 28, 6). Several of Menander's Indo-Greek successors inscribed the mention "Follower of the Dharma" in the Kharoshthi script on their coins, and depicted themselves or their divinities forming the *vitarka* mudra.

The interaction between Greek and Buddhist cultures may have had some influence on the evolution of Mahayana, as the faith developed its sophisticated philosophical approach and a man-god treatment of the Buddha somewhat reminiscent of Hellenic gods. It is also around that time that the first anthropomorphic representations of the Buddha are found, often in realistic Greco-Buddhist style: "One might regard the classical influence as including the general idea of representing a man-god in this purely human form, which was of course well familiar in the West, and it is very likely that the example of westerner's treatment of their gods was indeed an important factor in the innovation" (Boardman, "The Diffusion of Classical Art in Antiquity"). Central Asian Expansion

A Buddhist gold coin from India was found in northern Afghanistan at the archaeological site of Tillia Tepe, and dated to the 1st century CE. On the reverse, it depicts a lion with a nandipada, with the

Kharoshthi legend "Sih[o] vigatabhay[o]" ("The lion who dispelled fear"). On the obverse, an almost naked man only wearing an Hellenistic chlamys and a petasus hat (an iconography similar to that of Hermes/ Mercury) rolls a Buddhist wheel. The legend in Kharoshthi reads "Dharmacakrapravata[ko]" ("The one who turned the Wheel of the Law"). It has been suggested that this may be an early representation of the Buddha.

Rise of Mahayana (1st c. BCE–2nd c. CE)

The rise of Mahayana Buddhism from the 1st century BCE was accompanied by complex political changes in northwestern India. The Indo-Greek kingdoms were gradually overwhelmed, and their culture assimilated by the Indo-Scythians, and then the Yuezhi, who founded the Kushan Empire from around 12 BCE. The Kushans were supportive of Buddhism, and a fourth Buddhist council was convened by the Kushan emperor Kanishka, around 100 CE at Jalandhar or in Kashmir, and is usually associated with the formal rise of Mahayana Buddhism and its secession from Theravada Buddhism. Theravada Buddhism does not recognize the authenticity of this council, and it is sometimes called the "council of heretical monks".

The new form of Buddhism was characterized by an almost God-like treatment of the Buddha, by the idea that all beings have a Buddha-nature and should aspire to Buddhahood, and by a syncretism due to the various cultural influences within northwestern India and the Kushan Empire.

The Two Fourth Councils

The Fourth Council is said to have been convened in the reign of the Kushan emperor Kanishka, around 100 CE at Jalandhar or in Kashmir. Theravada Buddhism had its own Fourth Council in Sri Lanka. Therefore there are two Fourth Councils: one in Sri Lanka (Theravada), and one in Kashmir (Sarvastivadin).

It is said that for the Fourth Council of Kashmir, Kanishka gathered 500 monks headed by Vasumitra, partly, it seems, to compile extensive commentaries on the Abhidharma, although it is possible that some editorial work was carried out upon the existing canon itself. Allegedly, during the council there were all together three hundred thousand verses and over nine million statements compiled, and it took twelve years to complete. This council did not rely on the original Pali canon (the Tipitaka). Instead, a set of new scriptures was approved, as well as fundamental principles of Mahayana doctrine. The new scriptures, usually in the Gandhari vernacular and the Kharosthi script, were rewritten in the classical language of Sanskrit, to many scholars a turning point in the propagation of Buddhist thought. The main fruit of this Council was the redaction of Agamas and compilation of the vast commentary known as the Mahā-Vibhāshā ("Great Exegesis"), an extensive compendium and reference work on a portion of the Sarvâstivâdin Abhidharma.

Scholars believe that it was also around this time that a significant change was made in the language of the Sarvāstivādin canon, by converting an earlier Prakrit version into Sanskrit. Although this change was probably effected without significant loss of integrity to the canon, this event was of particular significance since Sanskrit was the official holy language of Brahmanism in India, and was also being used by other thinkers (regardless of their specific religious or philosophical allegiance), thus enabling a far wider audience to gain access to Buddhist ideas and practices. For this reason, all major (Mahayana) Buddhist scholars in India thereafter wrote their commentaries and treatises in Sanskrit. Therevada however never switched to Sanskrit, partly because Buddha explicitly forbade translation of his discourses into Sanskrit because it was an elitist religious language (like Latin was in Europe before). He wanted his monks to use a local language instead; a language which could be understood by all. Over time however, the language of the Theravadin scriptures (Pali) became a scholarly or elitist language as well.

Mahayana Expansion (1st c. CE–10th c. CE)

From that point on, and in the space of a few centuries, Mahayana was to flourish and spread in the East from India to South-East Asia, and towards the north to Central Asia, China, Korea, and finally to Japan in 538 CE.

India

After the end of the Kushans, Buddhism flourished in India during the dynasty of the Guptas (4th-6th century). Mahayana centers of learning were established, especially at Nalanda in north-eastern India, which was to become the largest and most influential Buddhist university for many centuries, with famous teachers such as Nagarjuna. The Gupta style of Buddhist art became very influential from South-East Asia to China as the faith was spreading there.

Indian Buddhism had weakened in the 6th century following the White Hun invasions and Mihirkulas persecution.

Huanzang reports in his travels across India during the 7th century of Buddhism being popular in Andhra, Dhanyakataka, and Dravida which today roughly correspond to the modern day Indian states of Andhra Pradesh and Tamil Nadu. While reporting many deserted stupas in the area around modern day Nepal and the persecution of buddhists by Ssanka in the Kingdom of Gouda. (In modern day West Bengal.) Xuanzang compliments the patronage of Harshavardana during the same period. After Harshavardanas kingdom, the rise of many small kingdoms that lead to the rise of the Rajputs across the gangetic plains and marked the end of Buddhist ruling clans along with a sharp decline in royal patronage until a revival under the Pala Empire in the Bengal region. Here Mahayana Buddhism flourished and spread to Bhutan and Sikkim between the 8th and the 12th century before the Palas collapsed under the assault of the Hindu Sena dynasty. The Palas created many temples and a distinctive school of Buddhist art. Xuanzang noted in his travels that in various regions Buddhism was giving way to Jainism and Hinduism.By the 10th century Buddhism had experienced a sharp decline beyond the Pala realms in Bengal under a resurgent Hinduism and the incorporation in Vaishnavite Hinduism of Buddha as the 9th incarnation of Vishnu.

A milestone in the decline of Indian Buddhism in the North occurred in 1193 when Turkic Islamic raiders under Muhammad Khilji burnt Nalanda. By the end of the 12th century, following the Islamic conquest of the Buddhist strongholds in Bihar, and the loss of political support coupled with social and caste pressures, the practice of Buddhism retreated to the Himalayan foothills in the North and Sri Lanka in the south. Additionally, the influence of Buddhism also waned due to Hinduism's revival movements such as Advaita, the rise of the bhakti movement and the missionary work of Sufis.

Central Asia

Central Asia had been influenced by Buddhism probably almost since the time of the Buddha. According to a legend preserved in Pali, the language of the Theravada canon, two merchant brothers from Bactria, named Tapassu and Bhallika, visited the Buddha and became his disciples. They then returned to Bactria and built temples to the Buddha (Foltz).

Central Asia long played the role of a meeting place between China, India and Persia. During the 2nd century BCE, the expansion of the Former Han to the west brought them into contact with the Hellenistic civilizations of Asia, especially the Greco-Bactrian Kingdoms. Thereafter, the expansion of Buddhism to the north led to the formation of Buddhist communities and even Buddhist kingdoms in the oases of Central Asia. Some Silk Road cities consisted almost entirely of Buddhist stupas and monasteries, and it seems that one of their main objectives was to welcome and service travelers between east and west.

The Theravada traditions first spread among the Turkic tribes before combining with the Mahayana forms during the 2nd and 3rd centuries BCE to cover modern-day Pakistan, Kashmir, Afghanistan, eastern and coastal Iran, Uzbekistan, Turkmenistan and Tajikistan. These were the ancient states of Gandhara, Bactria, Parthia and Sogdia from where it spread to China. Among the first of these Turkic tribes to adopt Buddhism was the Turki-Shahi who adopted Buddhism as early as the 3rd century BCE. It was not, however, the exclusive faith of this region. There were also Zoroastrians, Hindus, Nestorian Christians, Jews, Manichaeans, and followers of shamanism, Tengrism, and other indigenous, nonorganized systems of belief.

Various Nikaya schools persisted in Central Asia and China until around the 7th century CE. Mahayana started to become dominant during the period, but since the faith had not developed a Nikaya approach, Sarvastivadin and Dharmaguptakas remained the Vinayas of choice in Central Asian monasteries.

Various Buddhism kingdoms rose and prospered in both the Central Asian region and downwards into the Indian sub-continent such as Kushan Empire prior to the White Hun invasion in the 5th century where under the King Mihirkula they were heavily persecuted.

Buddhism in Central Asia started to decline with the expansion of Islam and the destruction of many stupas in war from the 7th century. The Muslims accorded them the status of dhimmis as "people of the Book", such as Christianity or Judaism and Al-Biruni wrote of Buddha as prophet "burxan".

Buddhism saw a surge during the reign of Mongols following the invasion of Genghis Khan and the establishment of the II Khanate and the Chagatai Khanate who brought their Buddhist influence with them during the 13th century, however within a 100 years the Mongols who remained in that region would convert to Islam and spread Islam across all the regions across central Asia. Only the eastern Mongols and the Mongols of the Yuan dynasty would keep Vajrayana Buddhism.

Parthia

Buddhism expanded westward into Arsacid Parthia, at least to the area of Merv, in ancient Margiana, today's territory of Turkmenistan. Soviet archeological teams have excavated in Giaur Kala, near Merv, a Buddhist chapel, a gigantic Buddha statue, as well as a monastery. Parthians were directly involved in the propagation of Buddhism: An Shigao (c. 148 CE), a Parthian prince, went to China, and is the first known translator of Buddhist scriptures into Chinese.

The eastern part of central Asia (Chinese, Turkestan, Tarim Basin, Xinjiang) has revealed extremely rich Buddhist works of art (wall paintings and reliefs in numerous caves, portable paintings on canvas, sculpture, ritual objects), displaying multiple influences from Indian and Hellenistic cultures. Serindian art is highly reminisçent of the Gandharan style, and scriptures in the Gandhari script Kharosthi have been found. Central Asians seem to have played a key role in the transmission of Buddhism to the East. The first translators of Buddhists scriptures into Chinese were either Parthian (Ch: Anxi) like An Shigao (c. 148 CE) or An Hsuan, Kushan of Yuezhi ethnicity like Lokaksema (c. 178 CE), Zhi Qian and Zhi Yao, or Sogdians like Kang Sengkai. Thirty-seven early translators of Buddhist texts are known, and the majority of them have been identified as Central Asians. Central Asian and East Asian Buddhist monks appear to have maintained strong exchanges until around the 10th century, as shown by frescoes from the Tarim Basin.

These influences were rapidly absorbed however by the vigorous Chinese culture, and a strongly Chinese particularism develops from that point.

Buddhism probably arrived in China around the 1st century CE from Central Asia (although there are some traditions about a monk visiting China during Ashoka's reign), and through to the 8th century it became an extremely active center of Buddhism.

First known Chinese Buddha statue, found in a late Han dynasty burial in Sichuan province. Circa 200 CE. The hair, the moustache and the clothing are strongly indicative of Gandharan influences ("Crossroads of Asia", p. 208)

The year 67 CE saw Buddhism's official introduction to China with the coming of the two monks Moton and Chufarlan. In 68 CE, under imperial patronage, they established the White Horse Temple which still exists today, close to the imperial capital at Luoyang. By the end of the second century, a prosperous community had been settled at Pengcheng (modern Xuzhou, Jiangsu).

The first known Mahayana scriptural texts are translations made into Chinese by the Kushan monk Lokaksema in Luoyang, between 178 and 189 CE. Some of the earliest known Buddhist artifacts found in China are small statues on "money trees", dated circa 200 CE, in typical Gandharan style (drawing): "That the imported images accompanying the newly arrived doctrine came from Gandhara is strongly suggested by such early Gandhara characteristics on this "money tree" Buddha as the high ushnisha, vertical arrangement of the hair, moustache, symmetrically looped robe and parallel incisions for the folds of the arms." ("Crossroads of Asia" p. 209)

Maitreya Buddha, Northern Wei, 443 CE

Buddhism flourished during the beginning of the Tang Dynasty (618–907). The dynasty was initially characterized by a strong openness to foreign influences, and renewed exchanges with Indian culture due to the numerous travels of Chinese Buddhist monks to India from the 4th to the 11th century. The Tang capital of Chang'an (today's Xi'an) became an important center for Buddhist thought. From there Buddhism spread to Korea, and Japanese embassies of Kentoshi helped gain footholds in Japan.

However foreign influences came to be negatively perceived towards the end of the Tang Dynasty. In the year 845, the Tang emperor Wu-Tsung outlawed all "foreign" religions (including Christian Nestorianism, Zoroastrianism, and Buddhism) in order to support the indigenous Taoism. Throughout his territory, he confiscated Buddhist possessions, destroyed monasteries and temples, and executed Buddhist monks, ending Buddhism's cultural and intellectual dominance. About a hundred years after the Great Anti-Buddhist Persecution, Buddhism revived during the Song Dynasty (1127–1279).

Pure Land and Chan Buddhism, however, continued to prosper for some centuries, the latter giving rise to Japanese Zen. In China, Chan flourished particularly under the Song dynasty (1127–1279), when its monasteries were great centers of culture and learning.

Today, China boasts one of the richest collections of Buddhist arts and heritages in the world. UNESCO World Heritage Sites such as the Mogao Caves near Dunhuang in Gansu province, the Longmen Grottoes near Luoyang in Henan province, the Yungang Grottoes near Datong in Shanxi province, and the Dazu Rock Carvings near Chongqing are among the most important and renowned Buddhist sculptural sites. The Leshan Giant Buddha, carved out of a hillside in the 8th century during Tang Dynasty and looking down on the confluence of three rivers, is still the largest stone Buddha statue in the world.

Korea

Buddhism was introduced around 372 CE, when Chinese ambassadors visited the Korean kingdom of Goguryeo, bringing scriptures and images. Buddhism prospered in Korea, and in particular Seon (Zen) Buddhism from the 7th century onward. However, with the beginning of the Confucean Yi Dynasty of the Joseon period in 1392, Buddhism was strongly discriminated against until it was almost completely eradicated, except for a remaining Seon movement.

Japan

Japan discovered Buddhism in the 6th century when Korean monks travelled to the islands together with numerous scriptures and works of art. The Buddhist religion was adopted by the state in the following century. Being geographically at the end of the Silk Road, Japan was able to preserve many aspects of Buddhism at the very time it was disappearing in India, and being suppressed in Central Asia and China. From 710 CE numerous temples and monasteries were built in the capital city of Nara, such as the five-story pagoda and Golden Hall of the Hōryū-ji, or the Kōfuku-ji temple. Countless paintings and sculptures were made, often under governmental sponsorship. The creation of Japanese Buddhist art was especially rich between the 8th and 13th century during the periods of Nara, Heian, and Kamakura. From the 12th and 13th, a further development was Zen art, following the introduction of the faith by Dogen and Eisai upon their return from China. Zen art is mainly characterized by original paintings (such as sumi-e and the Enso) and poetry (especially haikus), striving to express the true essence of the world through impressionistic and unadorned "non-dualistic" representations. The search for enlightenment "in the moment" also led to the development of other important derivative arts such as the Chanoyu tea ceremony or the Ikebana art of flower arrangement. This evolution went as far as considering almost any human activity as an art with a strong spiritual and aesthetic content, first and foremost in those activities related to combat techniques (martial arts).

Buddhism remains very active in Japan to this day. Around 80,000 Buddhist temples are preserved and regularly restored.

Southeast Asia

During the 1st century CE, the trade on the overland Silk Road tended to be restricted by the rise in the Middle-East of the Parthian empire, an unvanquished enemy of Rome, just as Romans were becoming extremely wealthy and their demand for Asian luxury was rising. This demand revived the sea connections between the Mediterranean and China, with India as the intermediary of choice. From that time, through trade connection, commercial settlements, and even political interventions, India started to strongly influence Southeast Asian countries. Trade routes linked India with southern Burma, central and southern Siam, lower Cambodia and southern Vietnam, and numerous urbanized coastal settlements were established there. For more than a thousand years, Indian influence was therefore the major factor that brought a certain level of cultural unity to the various countries of the region. The Pali and Sanskrit languages and the Indian script, together with Theravada and Mahayana Buddhism, Brahmanism, and Hinduism, were transmitted from direct contact and through sacred texts and Indian literature such as the Ramayana and the Mahabharata.

From the 5th to the 13th century, South-East Asia had very powerful empires and became extremely active in Buddhist architectural and artistic creation. The main Buddhist influence now came directly by sea from the Indian subcontinent, so that these empires essentially followed the Mahayana faith. The Sri Vijaya Empire to the south and the Khmer Empire to the north competed for influence, and their art expressed the rich Mahayana pantheon of the Bodhisattvas.

Vietnam

Srivijaya, a maritime empire centered at Palembang on the island of Sumatra in Indonesia, adopted Mahayana and Vajrayana

Buddhism under a line of rulers named the Sailendras. Yijing described Palembang as a great centre of Buddhist learning where the emperor supported over a thousand monks at his court. Atisha studied there before travelling to Tibet as a missionary. Sriviijaya spread Buddhist art during its expansion in Southeast Asia. Numerous statues of Bodhisattvas from this period are characterized by a very strong refinement and technical sophistication, and are found throughout the region. Extremely rich architectural remains are visible at the temple of Borobudur (the largest Buddhist structure in the world, built from around 780 CE), in Java, which has 505 images of the seated Buddha. Srivijaya declined due to conflicts with the Chola rulers of India, before being destabilized by the Islamic expansion from the 13th century.

Khmer Empire (9th–13th century)

Later, from the 9th to the 13th century, the Mahayana Buddhist and Hindu Khmer Empire dominated much of the South-East Asian peninsula. Under the Khmer, more than 900 temples were built in Cambodia and in neighboring Thailand. Angkor was at the center of this development, with a temple complex and urban organization able to support around one million urban dwellers. One of the greatest Khmer kings, Jayavarman VII (1181–1219), built large Mahayana Buddhist structures at Bayon and Angkor Thom.

Following the destruction of Buddhism in mainland India during the 11th century, Mahayana Buddhism declined in Southeast Asia, to be replaced by the introduction of Theravada Buddhism from Sri Lanka.

Emergence of the Vajrayana (5th century)

Vajrayāna Buddhism, also called Tantric Buddhism, first emerged in eastern India between the 5th and 7th centuries CE. It is sometimes considered a sub-school of Mahayana and sometimes a third major "vehicle" (*Yana*) of Buddhism in its own right. The Vajrayana is an extension of Mahayana Buddhism in that it does not offer new philosophical perspectives, but rather introduces additional techniques (upaya, or 'skilful means'), including the use of visualizations and other yogic practices. Many of the practices of Tantric Buddhism are common with Hindu tantricism (the usage of mantras, yoga, or the burning of sacrificial offerings). This school of thought was founded by Padmasambhava.

Early Vajrayana practitioners were forest-dwelling mahasiddas who lived on the margins of society, but by the 9th century Vajrayana had won acceptance at major Mahayana monastic universities such as Nalanda and Vikramshila. Along with much of the rest of Indian Buddhism, the Vajrayana was eclipsed in the wake of the late 12th century Muslim invasions. It has persisted in Tibet, where it was wholly transplanted from the 7th to 12th centuries and became the dominant form of Buddhism to the present day, and on a limited basis in Japan as well where it evolved into Shingon Buddhism.

Expansion of Buddhism to the West

After the Classical encounters between Buddhism and the West recorded in Greco-Buddhist art, information and legends about Buddhism seem to have reached the West sporadically. During the 8th century, Buddhist Jataka stories were translated into Syriac and Arabic as Kalilag and Damnag. An account of Buddha's life was translated in to Greek by John of Damascus, and widely circulated to Christians as the story of Barlaam and Josaphat. By the 1300s this story of Josaphat had become so popular that he was made a Catholic saint.

The next direct encounter between Europeans and Buddhism happened in Medieval times when the Franciscan friar William of Rubruck was sent on an embassy to the Mongol court of Mongke by the French king Saint Louis in 1253. The contact happened in Cailac (today's Qayaliq in Kazakhstan), and William originally thought they were wayward Christians (Foltz, "Religions of the Silk Road").

Major interest for Buddhism emerged during colonial times, when Western powers were in a position to witness the faith and its artistic manifestations in detail. European philosophy was strongly influenced by the study of oriental religions during that period. The opening of Japan in 1853 also created a considerable interest for the arts and culture of Japan, and provided access to one of the most thriving Buddhist cultures in the world. Buddhism started to enjoy a strong interest from the general population in the West following the turbulance of the 20th century.

Buddhism has been displaying a strong power of attraction, due to its tolerance, its lack of deist authority and determinism, and its focus on understanding reality through self inquiry. According to the latest census it is now the fastest growing religion in Great Britain.

EMPEROR ASHOKA (273-232 BC)

Asoka was the grandson of a great Indian military leader who set up the first large Indian empire. In the history of the world there have been thousands of kings and emperors who called themselves 'Their Highnesses', 'Their Majesties' and 'Their Exalted Majesties' and so on. They shone for a brief moment, and as quickly disappeared. But Ashoka shines and shines brightly like a bright star, even unto this day. So wrote H.G. Wells, British historian and noble seeker of the truth about mankind's tumultuous past.

Questionable Hereditary Succession

Ashoka was anointed the new emperor or ruler of the Mauryan Empire in 274 BCE. His grandfather, Chandragupta, had set out to conquer the weaker surrounding kingdoms to expand the territory of his people in 324 BCE, and was the first to rule over a unified India. Ashoka's father, Bindusara, established a reign much the same as his father's, controlling a larger kingdom than ever before known. When Bindusara became gravely ill, Ashoka succeeded him, although one hundred of his other brothers were mysteriously murdered. Many historians believe Ashoka had his own brothers eliminated so that he could succeed his father.

A Sudden Change of Heart

Ashoka's reign as emperor began with a series of wars and bloodshed, culminating in the Kalinga War of 260 BC. The mammoth loss of life and suffering witnessed on the battlefield made him turn away from war. He subsequently became deeply influenced by Buddhism, and adopted the dharma, which consists of basic virtuous teachings that can be practiced by all men regardless of social origins. "Dharma" is derived from the Sanskrit word for "duty".

Kalinga War

Ashokan Empire 250 BC Map

Chandragupta's son Bindusara followed the footprints of his father in his political lines and conquered more territories except the kingdom of Kalinga (parts of what is modern Orissa). Historians point out that the empire Bindusara ruled over had almost the form and extent of modern India. He was succeeded by his son Ashoka, hailed till date as the most famous of all Indian emperors. The fierce war he waged with Kalinga to annex it caused untold miseries and bloodshed and deaths and it made him sit back and think about the futility of war. After the annexation of Kalinga, in an edict on the war, Ashoka declared that 150,000 prisoners were taken and more than 100,000 men killed. But after the war the king had a total change of mind, turned to the Buddhist teachings and became a Buddhist to become the greatest follower and propagator of the religion. He was instrumental in the spreading of Buddhism all over South Asia and South East Asia. The Mauryan Empire and its power reached its peak under Ashoka's rule. It had become one of the largest empires in the whole of the East.

Historians point out that Ashoka's empire extended in the West up to Arachosia (now part of Afghanistan). An edict of Ashoka was found in Lampaka (near modern Jelalabad) which confirmed that Paropamisus actually was part of the Mauryan empire. Data found in the Kashmir chronicle Rajatarangini and in descriptions by Chinese pilgrims give us reason to believe that part of Kashmir was also incorporated into Ashoka's empire. Parts of Nepal, and Bengal were also part of his empire, as suggested by epigraphic evidence.

Towards a New Imperial Unity

Ashoka saw the dharma as a righteous path showing the utmost respect for all living things. The dharma would bring harmony and unity to India in the form of much needed compassion.

Serving as a guiding light, a voice of conscious that is the dharma can lead one to be a respectful and highly responsible human being. Edward D'Cruz interprets the Ashokan dharma as a "religion to be used as a symbol of a new imperial unity and a cementing force to weld the diverse and heterogeneous elements of the empire". Ashoka's intent was to instigate "a practice of social behaviour so broad and benevolent in its scope that no person, no matter what his religion, could reasonably object to it".

The Moral Order of Dharma

Ashoka's dream was to unify a nation so large that its people of one region shared little in common with those of another region. Diversity of religion, ethnicity and many cultural aspects held citizens against each other, creating social barriers. The moral order of dharma could be agreed upon as beneficial and progressive by all who could understand its merits; in fact, the dharma had long been a primary practice for members of Hinduism, Jainism and Buddhism. Dharma became the link between king and commoner; everyone lived by the same law of moral, religious and civil obligations towards others.

Pillars of the Earth

Ashokan Pillar-3

The reign of Ashoka Mauryan could easily have disappeared into history as the ages passed by, and would have, if hadn't he left behind a record of his trials. The testimony of this wise king was discovered in the form of magnificently sculpted pillars and boulders with the various actions and teachings he wished to be published etched into the stone. What Ashoka left behind was the first written language in India since the ancient city of Harrapa. Rather than Sanskrit, the language used for inscription was the current spoken form called Prakrita. In translating these monuments, historians learn the bulk of what is assumed to have been true fact of the Mauryan Empire. It is difficult to determine whether or not some actual events ever happened, but the stone etchings clearly depict how Ashoka wanted to be thought of and remembered.

The Emperor's New Edicts

King Ashoka, the third monarch of the Indian Mauryan dynasty, has come to be regarded as one of the most exemplary rulers in

Rock Edict of Ashoka at *Shahbazgarhi*

world history. Although Buddhist literature preserved the legend of this ruler—the story of a cruel and ruthless king who converted to Buddhism and thereafter established a reign of virtue - definitive historical records of his reign were lacking. Then in the nineteenth century there came to light a large number of edicts, in India, Nepal, Pakistan and Afghanistan.

These edicts, inscribed on rocks and pillars, proclaim Asoka's reforms and policies and promulgate his advice to his subjects. The present rendering of these edicts, based on earlier translations, offers us insights into a powerful and capable ruler's attempt to establish an empire on the foundation of righteousness, a reign which makes the moral and spiritual welfare of his subjects its primary concern.

Beyond Greed, Hatred and Delusion

We have no way of knowing how effective Ashoka's reforms were or how long they lasted, but we do know that monarchs throughout the ancient Buddhist world were encouraged to look to his style of good government as an ideal to be venerated and kindredly administered. King Ashoka undoubtedly has to be credited with the first serious attempt to develop a Buddhist polity. Today, with widespread disillusionment in prevailing ideologies, and the search for a political philosophy that goes beyond greed (capitalism), hatred (communism) and delusion (dictatorships led by "infallible" leaders), Ashoka's edicts may still make a meaningful contribution to the development of a more spiritually-based political system of good government for every nation on earth.

A Well Respected Man

Emperor Ashoka was a cruel and merciless ruler at first. He waged war on his perceived enemies on a whim, and caused much suffering amongst his own people. While observing a massive slaughter at the front lines of his army, he experienced a change of heart and turned to the welfare of his own people, who still justly feared him as a ruthless and highly oppressive tyrant. Somewhere along the way he had become a Buddhist, and as a result taught and persuaded his people to love and respect all living things. He insisted on the recognition of the sanctity of all human life. The horrors of war have often transformed savage hearts into compassionate ones. Even the unnecessary slaughter or mutilation of animals was immediately abolished. Wildlife became protected by the king's law against sport hunting and branding. Limited hunting was permitted for consumption reasons but the overwhelming majority of Indians chose by their own free will to become vegetarians. Ashoka also showed mercy to those imprisoned, allowing them leave for the outside a day of the year. He attempted to raise the professional ambition of the common man by building universities for study and water transit and irrigation systems for trade and agriculture. He treated his subjects as equals regardless of their religion, politics and cast. The kingdoms surrounding his, so easily overthrown, were instead made to be well-respected allies.

In His Own Words

All men are my children. I am like a father to them. As every father desires the good and the happiness of his children, I wish that all men should be happy always.

Coda

During his reign, Ashoka became an avid Buddhist practitioner, building 84,000 stupas across his empire to house the sacred relics of the Lord Buddha. He sent his family on religious pilgrimages to foreign places, and staged massive assemblies so holy men from the world over could converse upon the philosophies of the day. More than even Buddhism was Ashoka's deep involvement in the dharma. The dharma became the ultimate expression of the moral and ethical standards he desired his subjects to live by. Ashoka defined the main principles of dharma (dhamma) as nonviolence, tolerance of all sects and opinions, obedience to parents, respect for the Brahmans and other religious teachers and priests, liberality towards friends, humane treatment of servants, and generosity towards all. These principles suggest a general ethic of behaviour to which no religious or social group could object.

In perhaps a fitting tribute to this great man of vision and unity, the Indian Government has adopted the famous lion capital from his pillar at Sarnath as its official national emblem. The wheel design on the capital's base has also become the central figure of the nation's flag. May the wheel keep on turning for the sake of all men who are brothers in this brave new millennium of ours, and may the teachings of the Light of Asia continue to reach every corner of the earth despite what some inferior men may do or say.

3
Central Idea of Buddhism

Buddhist Religion

Buddhism is a path of practice and spiritual development, providing a person with insight into the true nature of life. Buddhist practices, such as meditation, serve as the means of changing oneself, in order to develop the qualities of awareness, kindness, and wisdom. Buddhism is not about teaching or learning, but about experiencing.

Buddhist ideology does not advocate the practice of worshipping God in a physical form. Hence, quite often, it is not really seen as a religion in the normal sense. The basic tenets of Buddhist teaching are straightforward and practical - nothing is fixed or permanent; actions have consequences; change is possible. It teaches practical methods, such as meditation, which enable people to realize and utilize its teachings in order to transform their experience. They are taught to be fully responsible for their lives and to develop the qualities of wisdom and compassion.

There are over 360 million followers of Buddhism in the world. Even though they follow different forms of Buddhism, their traditions are characterized by the same values of non-violence, lack of dogma, tolerance of differences, and usually, by the practice of meditation.

Meditation

Meditation is at the heart of the Buddhist way of life. It basically helps you in to attain a higher level of consciousness. We first learn to identify our negative mental state known as 'delusion', and then develop peaceful and positive mental state or 'virtuous mind'.

We overcome our delusions by becoming familiar with our virtuous mind. Later, we have to maintain the virtuous minds we have developed and use our wisdom to solve the problems of daily life. As our mind becomes more positive, our actions become more constructive and our experience of life becomes more satisfying and beneficial to others.

Anyone can learn basic meditation techniques and experience great benefits. However, the progress beyond basic meditation requires faith in the Three Jewels - Buddha, Dharma and Sangha. It is usually seen that this develops naturally as people experience the benefits of their meditation practice.

The Spiritual Path

The teachings of Buddha reveal a step-by-step path to lasting happiness. By following this path, anyone can gradually transform his or her mind from its present confused and self-centered state to the blissful mind of a Buddha.

It is said that: "Every living being has the potential to become a Buddha, someone who has completely purified his or her mind of all faults and limitations and has brought all good qualities to perfection. Our mind is like a cloudy sky, in essence clear and pure but overcast by the clouds of delusions."

Just as the thickest clouds eventually disperse, even the heaviest delusions can be removed from our mind. Delusions such as hatred, greed, and ignorance are not an intrinsic part of the mind. If we apply the appropriate methods, they can be completely eliminated and we will experience the supreme happiness of full enlightenment.

After attaining enlightenment, we will have all the necessary qualities - universal love and compassion, omniscient wisdom and boundless spiritual power - to lead all living beings to the same exalted state. This is the ultimate aim of Mahayana Buddhism.

India, being the birthplace of Gautam Buddha, figures as one of the most important places in Buddhism.

Divisions

The most frequently used classification of present-day Buddhism among scholars divides present-day adherents into the following three traditions or geographical or cultural areas: Theravada, East Asian Buddhism and Tibetan Buddhism.

An alternative scheme used by some scholars has two divisions, Theravada and Mahayana. In this classification, Mahayana includes both East Asian and Tibetan Buddhism. This scheme is the one ordinarily used in the English language. Some scholars use other schemes. Buddhists themselves have a variety of other schemes.

Buddhism Today

Buddhism had become virtually extinct in India, and although it continued to exist in surrounding countries, its influence was no longer expanding. It is now again gaining strength. While estimates of the number of Buddhist followers range from 230 to 500 million worldwide, most estimates are between 310 million, and 350 million. In addition, most scholars classify similar numbers of people under a category they call variously Chinese (folk/traditional) religion, which is an amalgam of various traditions, including Buddhism. Furthermore, estimates are uncertain because of difficulties in defining who counts as a Buddhist; According to one analysis, Buddhism is the fourth-largest religion in the world behind Christianity, Islam, and Hinduism. The monks' order (Sangha), which began during the lifetime of the Buddha in India, is among the oldest organizations on earth.

Theravāda Buddhism, using Pāli as its scriptural language, is the dominant form of Buddhism in Cambodia, Laos, Thailand, Sri Lanka, and Burma. Also the Dalit Buddhist movement in India (inspired by B. R. Ambedkar) practices Theravada.

East Asian forms of Mahayana Buddhism that use scriptures in Chinese are dominant in most of China, Japan, Korea, Taiwan, Singapore and Vietnam as well as within Chinese and Japanese communities within Indochina, Southeast Asia and the West.

Tibetan Buddhism, using the Tibetan language, is found in Tibet, and the surrounding areas in India, Bhutan, Mongolia, Nepal, and the Russian Federation

Most Buddhist groups in the West are at least nominally affiliated to some eastern tradition listed above. An exception is the Friends of the Western Buddhist Order, though they can be considered Mahayanist in a broad sense.

According to a website specializing in religious statistics, the numbers of adherents of the three main traditions listed above are about 124, 185 and 20 million, respectively.

At the present time, the teachings of all three branches of Buddhism have spread throughout the world, and Buddhist texts are increasingly translated into local languages. While, in the West, Buddhism is often seen as exotic and progressive, in the East, Buddhism is regarded as familiar and part of the establishment. Buddhists in Asia are frequently well organized and well funded. In a number of countries, it is recognized as an official religion and receives state support. In the West, Buddhism is recognized as one of the growing spiritual influences.

Some Teachings

In Theravada Buddhism, any person who has awakened from the "sleep of ignorance" (by directly realizing the true nature of reality), without instruction, and teaches it to others is called a Buddha, while those who achieve realisations but do not teach others are called *paccekabuddhas*. All traditional Buddhists agree that Shakyamuni or Gotama Buddha was not the only Buddha: it is generally taught that there have been many past Buddha's and that there will be future Buddhas too. If a person achieves this awakening, he or she is called an *arahant*. Siddhartha Gautama, the Buddha, is thus only one among other Buddha's before or after him. His teachings are oriented toward the attainment of this kind of awakening, also called liberation, or Nirvana.

One of the teachings ascribed to the Buddha regarding the holy life and the goal of liberation is constituted by the "The Four Noble Truths", which focus on dukkha, a term that refers to suffering or the unhappiness ultimately characteristic of unawakened, worldly life. According to the interpretation of earlier Western scholars, followed by many modern Theravadins, the Four Noble Truths regarding suffering state what is its nature, its cause, its cessation, and the way leading to its cessation. This way to the cessation of suffering is called "The Noble Eightfold Path". However, according to at least some recent scholars, the so-called truths are not statements at all, but "things": suffering and the rest.

Numerous distinct groups have developed since the passing of the Buddha, with diverse teachings that vary widely in practice, philosophical emphasis, and culture. Few valid generalizations are possible about all Buddhists.

Middle Way

An important guiding principle of Buddhist practice is the Middle Way which was discovered by the Buddha prior to his enlightenment (bodhi). The Middle Way or Middle Path has several definitions:

It is often described as the practice of non-extremism; a path of moderation away from the extremes of self-indulgence and opposing self-mortification. It also refers to taking a middle ground between certain metaphysical views, e.g. that things ultimately either exist or do not exist.

An explanation of the state of Nirvana and perfect enlightenment where all dualities fuse and cease to exist as separate entities.

Refuge in the Three Jewels

Traditionally, the first step in most forms of Buddhism requires taking refuge, as the foundation of one's religious practice, in Buddhism's Three Jewels .They are:

The Buddha (i.e., Awakened One). This is a title for those who attained Awakening similar to the Buddha and helped others to attain it. See also the Tathāgata and Śākyamuni Buddha. The Buddha could also be represented as the wisdom that understands

Dharma, and in this regard the Buddha represents the perfect wisdom that sees reality in its true form.

The Dharma: The teachings or law as expounded by the Buddha. Dharma also means the law of nature based on behaviour of a person and its consequences to be experienced (action and reaction). It can also (especially in Mahayana Buddhism) connote the ultimate and sustaining Reality which is in severable from the Buddha.

The Sangha: This term literally means "group" or "congregation," but when it is used in Buddhist teaching the word refers to one of two very specific kinds of groups: either the community of Buddhist monastics (bhikkhus and bhikkhunis), or the community of people who have attained at least the first stage of Awakening (Sotapanna (pali)—one who has entered the stream to enlightenment). According to some modern Buddhists, it also consists of laymen and laywomen, the caretakers of the monks, those who have accepted parts of the monastic code but who have not been ordained as monks or nuns.

According to the scriptures, The Buddha presented himself as a model, however, he did not ask his followers simply to have faith in his example of a human who escaped the pain and danger of existence. In addition, he encouraged them to put his teachings to the test and accept what they could verify on their own. The Dharma, i.e. the teaching of the Buddha, offers a refuge by providing guidelines for the alleviation of suffering and the attainment of enlightenment. The Sangha (Buddhist Order of monks) is considered to provide a refuge by preserving the authentic teachings of the Buddha and providing further examples that the truth of the Buddha's teachings is attainable.

In the Mahayana, the Buddha tends not to be viewed as merely human, but as the earthly projection of a being beyond the range and reach of thought. Moreover, in certain Mahayana sutras, the Buddha, Dharma and Sangha are viewed essentially as one: all three are seen as the eternal Buddha himself.

Many Buddhists believe that there is no otherworldly salvation from one's karma. The suffering caused by the karmic effects of previous thoughts, words and deeds can be alleviated by following the Noble Eightfold Path, although the Buddha of some Mahayana sutras, such as the Lotus Sutra, the Angulimaliya Sutra and the Nirvana Sutra, also teaches that powerful sutras such as the above-named can, through the very act of their being heard or recited, wholly expunge great swathes of negative karma.

The Four Noble Truths

According to Lord Buddha the sooner a man realizes the four noble truths, the better. They are:

"The noble truth that is suffering"
"The noble truth that is the arising of suffering"
"The noble truth that is the end of suffering"
"The noble truth that is the way leading to the end of suffering"

Simply put,

There is suffering
There is a cause of suffering — craving
There is the cessation of suffering — Nirvana
There is a way leading to the cessation of suffering — the Noble Eightfold Path

According to the scriptures, the Four Noble Truths were among the topics of the first sermon given by the Buddha after his enlightenment, which was given to the five ascetics with whom he had practiced austerities. The Four Noble Truths were originally spoken by the Buddha not in the form of a religious or philosophical text, but in the manner of a medical diagnosis and remedial prescription in a style that was common at that time. The early teaching and the traditional understanding in the Theravada is that these are an advanced teaching for those who are ready for them. The Mahayana position is that they are a preliminary teaching for people not yet ready for the higher and more expansive Mahayana teachings.

The Noble Eightfold Path

The eight-spoked Dharmacakra. The eight spokes represent the Noble Eightfold Path of Buddhism.

The Noble Eightfold Path is the way to the cessation of suffering, the fourth part of the Four Noble Truths. This is divided into three sections: Śīla (which concerns wholesome physical actions), Samadhi (which concerns the meditative concentration of the mind) and Prajñā (which concerns spiritual insight into the true nature of all things). The Noble Eightfold Path are:

Right Speech—One speaks in a non hurtful, not exaggerated, truthful way.

Right Actions—Wholesome action, avoiding action that would do harm.

Right Livelihood—One's way of livelihood does not harm in any way oneself or others; directly or indirectly.

Samadhi is developing mastery over one's own mind. Within this division are another three parts of the Noble Eightfold Path:

Right Effort/Exercise—One makes an effort to improve.

Right Mindfulness/Awareness—Mental ability to see things for what they are with clear consciousness.

Right Concentration/Meditation—Being aware of the present reality within oneself, without any craving or aversion.

Prajña is the wisdom which purifies the mind. Within this division fall two more parts of the Noble Eightfold Path:

Right Understanding—Understanding reality as it is, not just as it appears to be.

Right Thoughts—Change in the pattern of thinking.

Buddhist Texts

Buddhist scriptures and other texts exist in great variety. Different schools of Buddhism place varying levels of value on them. Some schools venerate certain texts as religious objects in themselves, while others take a more scholastic approach. The Buddhist canon of scripture is known in Sanskrit as the Tripitaka and in Pāli as the Tipitaka. These terms literally mean "three baskets" and refer to the three main divisions of the canon, which are:

The Vinaya Pitaka, containing disciplinary rules for the Sanghas of Buddhist monks and nuns, as well as a range of other texts including explanations of why and how rules were instituted, supporting material, and doctrinal clarification.

The Sūtra Pitaka (Pāli: Sutta Pitaka), contains the actual discourses of the Buddha.

The Abhidharma Pitaka (Pāli: Abhidhamma Pitaka) contains commentaries or systematic expositions of the Buddha's teachings.

According to the scriptures, soon after the death of the Buddha, the first Buddhist council was held; a monk named Mahākāśyapa (Pāli: Mahākassapa) presided. The goal of the council was to record the Buddha's sayings—sūtras (Sanskrit) or suttas (Pāli)—and codify monastic rules (Vinaya). Ānanda, the Buddha's personal attendant, was called upon to recite the discourses of the Buddha, and according to some sources the abhidhamma, and Upāli, another disciple, recited the rules of the Vinaya. These became the basis of the Tripitaka. However, this record was initially transmitted orally in form of chanting, and was committed to text in a much later period. Both the sūtras and the Vinaya of every Buddhist school contain a wide variety of elements including discourses on the Dharma, commentaries on other teachings, cosmological and cosmogonical texts, stories of the Buddha's previous lives, and lists relating to various subjects.

The Theravāda and other Early Buddhist Schools traditionally believe that the texts of their canon contain the actual words of the Buddha. The Theravāda canon, also known as the Pāli Canon after the language it was written in, contains some four million words. Other texts, such as the Mahāyāna sūtras, are also considered by some to be the word of the Buddha, but supposedly either were transmitted in secret, or via lineages of mythical beings (such as the nāgas), or came directly from other Buddhas or bodhisattvas. Some six hundred Mahāyāna sutras have survived in Sanskrit or in Chinese or Tibetan translations.

The followers of Theravāda Buddhism take the scriptures known as the Pāli Canon as definitive and authoritative, while the followers of Mahāyāna Buddhism base their faith and philosophy primarily on the Mahāyāna sūtras and their own versions of the Vinaya. The Pāli sutras, along with other, closely-related scriptures, are known to the other schools as the āgamas.

Whereas the Theravādins adhere solely to the Pāli canon and its commentaries, the adherents of Mahāyāna accept both the agamas and the Mahāyāna sūtras as authentic and valid teachings of the Buddha, designed for different types of persons and different levels of spiritual penetration. For the Theravādins, however, the Mahayana sûtras are works of poetic fiction, not the words of the Buddha himself. The Theravadins are confident that the Pali canon represents the full and final statement by the Buddha of his Dhamma—and nothing more is truly needed beyond that. Anything added which claims to be the word of the Buddha and yet is not found in the Canon or its commentaries is treated with extreme caution if not outright rejection by Theravada.

For the Mahāyānists, in contrast, the âgamas do indeed contain basic, foundational, and, therefore, relatively weighty pronouncements of the Buddha, but from the Mahayana standpoint the Mahāyāna sutras articulate the Buddha's higher, more advanced and deeper doctrines, reserved for those who follow the Bodhisattva path. That path is explained to be built upon the motivation to achieve not only personal liberation, but Buddhahood itself in order to know how best to liberate all living beings from unhappiness. Hence the name Mahāyāna (lit., the Great Vehicle), which has room for both the general masses of sentient beings and those who are more developed. The "Great" of "Maha-yana" is indeed typical of much of this version of Buddhism—from the physical bigness (lengthiness) of some of the Mahayana sutras and the vastness of the Bodhisattva vow (to strive for all future time to help free all other persons and creatures from pain), to the (in some sutras and Tantras) final attainment of the Buddha's "Great Self" (mahatman) in the sphere of "Great

Nirvana" (mahanirvana). For Theravadins and many scholars, however, the self-proclaimed "greatness" of the Mahayana Sutras does not make them a true account of the life and teachings of Gautama Buddha.

Unlike many religions, Buddhism has no single central text that is universally referred to by all traditions. However, scholars have referred to the Vinaya Pitaka and the first four Nikayas of the Sutta Pitaka as the common core of all Buddhist traditions. This could, however, be considered misleading, as Mahāyāna considers these not a core, merely a preliminary teaching, and the Tibetans never even translated most of the âgamas, though theoretically recognizing them. The size and complexity of the Buddhist canons have been seen by some (including Buddhist social reformer Babasaheb Ambedkar) as presenting barriers to the wider understanding of Buddhist philosophy.

Over the years, various attempts have been made at synthesizing a single Buddhist text that will encompass all of the major principles of Buddhism. In the Theravada tradition, condensed 'study texts' were created that combined popular or influential scriptures into single volumes that could be studied by novice monks. Later in Sri Lanka, the Dhammapada was championed as a unifying scripture.

4

Vipassana—The Path to Salvation

Vipassana Meditation – The Technique

Vipassana, which means to see things as they really are, is one of India's most ancient techniques of meditation. *It was rediscovered by Gautama Buddha* more than 2500 years ago and was taught by him as a universal remedy for universal ills, i.e., an Art of Living.

This non-sectarian technique aims for the total eradication of mental impurities and the resultant highest happiness of full liberation. Healing, not merely the curing of diseases, but the essential healing of human suffering, is its purpose.

Vipassana is a way of self-transformation through self-observation. It focuses on the deep interconnection between mind and body, which can be experienced directly by disciplined attention to the physical sensations that form the life of the body, and that continuously interconnect and condition the life of the mind. It is this observation-based, self-exploratory journey to the common root of mind and body that dissolves mental impurity, resulting in a balanced mind full of love and compassion.

The scientific laws that operate one's thoughts, feelings, judgments and sensations become clear. Through direct experience, the nature of how one grows or regresses, how one produces suffering or frees oneself from suffering is understood. Life becomes characterized by increased awareness, non-delusion, self-control and peace.

The Tradition

Since the time of Buddha, Vipassana has been handed down, to the present day, by an unbroken chain of teachers. Although Indian by descent, the current teacher in this chain, Mr. S.N. Goenka, was born and raised in Burma (Myanmar). While living there he had the good fortune to learn Vipassana from his teacher, Sayagyi U Ba Khin who was at the time a high Government official. After receiving training from his teacher for fourteen years, Mr. Goenka settled in India and began teaching Vipassana in 1969. Since then he has taught tens of thousands of people of all races and all religions in both the East and West. In 1982 he began to appoint assistant teachers to help him meet the growing demand for Vipassana courses.

The Courses

The technique is taught at ten-day residential courses during which participants follow a prescribed Code of Discipline, learn the basics of the method, and practice sufficiently to experience its beneficial results. The course requires hard, serious work. There are three steps to the training. The first step is, for the period of the course, to abstain from killing, stealing, sexual activity, speaking falsely, and intoxicants. This simple code of moral conduct serves to calm the mind, which otherwise would be too agitated to perform the task of self-observation.

The next step is to develop some mastery over the mind by learning to fix one's attention on the natural reality of the ever changing flow of breath as it enters and leaves the nostrils. By the fourth day the mind is calmer and more focused, better able to undertake the practice of Vipassana itself: observing sensations throughout the body, understanding their nature, and developing equanimity by learning not to react to them.

Finally, on the last full day participants learn the meditation of loving kindness or goodwill towards all, in which the purity developed during the course is shared with all beings.

The entire practice is actually a mental training. Just as we use physical exercises to improve our bodily health, Vipassana can be used to develop a healthy mind.

Because it has been found to be genuinely helpful, great emphasis is put on preserving the technique in its original, authentic form. It is not taught commercially, but instead is offered freely. No person involved in its teaching receives any material remuneration.

There are no charges for the courses - not even to cover the cost of food and accommodation. All expenses are met by donations from people who, having completed a course and experienced the benefits of Vipassana, wish to give others the opportunity to benefit from it also.

Of course, the results come gradually through continued practice. It is unrealistic to expect all problems to be solved in ten days. Within that time, however, the essentials of Vipassana can be learned so that it can be applied in daily life. The more the technique is practiced, the greater the freedom from misery, and the closer the approach to the ultimate goal of full liberation. Even ten days can provide results which are vivid and obviously beneficial in everyday life. All sincere people are welcome to join a Vipassana course to see for themselves how the technique works and to measure the benefits. All those who try it will find Vipassana to be an invaluable tool with which to achieve and share real happiness with others.

Principal Meditation Centres in India

Dhamma Giri Meditation Centre Igatpuri, Maharashtra

Dhamma Pattana Meditation Centre Gorai, Mumbai, Maharashtra

Dhamma Tapovana Long Course Centre Igatpuri, Maharashtra

Apart from this Vipassana Sadhna Sansthan has 44 centres in India and 188 centres all over world spread across 5 continents.

Vandana (The Buddhist Prayer)

Nammo Tasso Bhagawato Arahato
Samma Sambuddhassa

Nammo Tasso Bhagawato Arahato
Samma Sambuddhassa

Nammo Tasso Bhagawato Arahato
Samma Sambuddhassa

Honour to him,
The blessed one,
The Worthy one,
The fully Enlightened one.

Ti-Sarana

Buddham saranam gacchami
Dhammam saranam gacchami
Sangham saranam gachhami

Dutiyampi Buddham saranam gacchami
Dutiyampi Dhammam saranam gacchami
Dutiyampi Sangham saranam gacchami

Tatiyampi Buddham saranam gacchami
Tatiyampi Dhamam saranam gacchami
Tatiyampi Sangham saranam gacchami

I go to the Buddha as my refuge.
I go to the Dhamma as my refuge.
I go to the Sangha as my refuge.

For the second time
I go to the Buddha as my refuge.
For the second time
I go to the Dhamma as my refuge.
For the second time
I go to the Sangha as my refuge.
For the third time
I go to the Buddha as my refuge.
For the third time
I go to the Dhamma as my refuge.
For the third time
I go to the Sangha as my refuge.

Panca Sila

Panati-pata
Veramani sikkha padam samadiyami
Adinna-dana
Veramani sikkha padam samadiyami
Kamesu miccha-cara
Veramani sikkha padam samadiyami
Musavada
Veramani sikkha padam samadiyami
Sura meraya-majja-pama-datthana
Veramani sikkha padama samadiyami

I take the precept to
Abstain from destroying living beings.
I take the precept to
Abstain from taking things not given.

I take the precept to
Abstain from sexual misconduct.
I take the precept to
Abstain from false speech.
I take the precept to
Abstain from taking anything that
Causes intoxication or heedlessness.

Salutation to the Buddha

Iti pi so Bhagava Araham
Samma sambuddho
vijja Carana-sampanno
Sugato Lokavidu Anuttaro
Purisa damma-sarathi
Sattha Deva-manussanam
Buddho Bhagava ti

Such indeed is the blessed one, exalted,
Omniscient, endowed with knowledge and virtues.
Gone beyond, knower of the worlds,
A guide incomparable for the training of individuals.
Teachers of gods and men,
Enlightened and Holy.

Salutation to the Dhamma

Svakkhato Bhagavata Dhammo
Sanditthiko Akaliko
Ehi – passiko Opanayiko
Paccattam veditabbo vinnuhi ti

Well expounded in the Dhamma
By the Blessed One,
To be self- realised;
To be but approached to be seen;
Capable of being entered upon;
To be attained by the wise, each by himself.

Salutation to the Sangha

Supatipanno Bhagavato
Savaka sangho

Uju patipanno Bhagavato
Savaka sangho
Naya patipanno Bhagavato

Savaka sangho
Samici patipanno Bhagavato
Savaka sangho
Yadidam cattari purisa yugani
Attha purisa puggala
Essa bhagavato savaka sangho
Ahuneyyo pahuneyyo
Dakkhineyyo anjali karaniyo
Anuttaram punnak khettam lokassa ti

Of good conduct is the Order
Of the Diciples of the Blessed One.
Of upright conduct is the Order
Of the Diciples of the Blessed One.
Of wise conduct is the Order
Of the Disciples of the Blessed One.
Of dutiful conduct is the Order
Of the Disciples of the Blessed One.
This Order of the Disciples of
the Blessed One, namely,
these four Pairs of Persons,
is worthy of offerings,
is worthy of hospitality,
is worthy of gifts,
is worthy of reverential saluation,
is an incomparable field of merits
to the World.

5
Places Associated with Buddhism—Caves

Buddhist Caves

Ajanta Caves

The Ajanta caves are situated in the Aurangabad district of Maharashtra, India. The caves, thirty in number, are said to have witnessed the prosperity as well as the decline of the two sects of Buddhism, the Hinayana and the Mahayana.

They are adorned with paintings, scriptures and architecture of both the sects.

Ajanta caves served as the residence of the Buddhist monks and religious devotees for more than 800 years. Today, these caves hold the distinction of being declared a World Heritage Site by UNESCO. Ajanta Caves signify the transition from the Hinayana sect of Buddhism to the Mahayana sect of Buddhism. The Hinayana sect made use of the stupas and other rock forms to represent Buddha. On the other hand, Mahayana sect used idols. Cave number 8, 9, 10, 12, 13 and 15 belong to Hinayana, the older sect. While, those of number 1, 2, 16, 17, 19 and 26 are related to Mahayana sect. The 19th and 26th caves are Chaityas. Some of the caves have not been finished till date.

Bodhisattva-Ajanta Cave Painting

Cave number nine, ten, twelve and thirteen were prepared in the first phase and date back to somewhere between 2nd century BC and 1st century BC.

Cave number nine and ten comprise of the Chaitya Halls or shrines. Cave number twelve and thirteen basically served as viharas or monasteries. The second phase came up with cave number one to seven, eleven and fourteen to twenty-nine. All of these caves date back to somewhere between 5th century AD to 6th century AD.

Cave number nineteen, twenty six and twenty-nine comprise of Chaitya Halls or shrines. While, cave number one to seven, eleven, fourteen to eighteen, twenty to twenty-five, Twenty-seven and twenty-eight are viharas or monasteries. Cave number two, three, five, eight, twenty-three to twenty-five and twenty-eight are still unfinished. Many caves are adorned with sculptures depict Buddha preaching in a sitting position.

Ellora Caves

Three-storied Buddhist School in Ellora

Ellora Caves are situated in the state of Maharashtra, India. They lie at a distance of approximately 25 km from the Aurangabad district. The beautiful caves of Ellora symbolize three of the major religions of the world, namely Buddhism, Hinduism and Jainism. They also hold the distinction of being declared a World Heritage Site by UNESCO.

Ellora Caves, cut out of the vertical face of a cliff, comprise of splendid chaityas (halls of worship), viharas (monasteries) and Hindu and Jain temples. There are a total of 34 monasteries and temples inside these caves. All of them date back to somewhere between 5th century AD and 11th century AD and have been built in a linear pattern. All the caves have different religious inclinations. Twelve of the caves (cave number 1 to 12) belong to the Mahayana sect of Buddhism and were built between 550 AD and 750 AD. Seventeen caves (cave number 13 to 29) comprise of Hindu temples and were constructed between 600 AD and 875 AD. Five caves (cave number 30 to 34) belong to the Jains and were built between 800 AD and 1000 AD. Some time back, archaeologists unearthed 22 more caves at Ellora, devoted to Lord Shiva, a Hindu God.

The Kailash Temple (Cave 16), built c.770-870 AD

All the caves are adorned with magnificent paintings and sculptures. The Buddhist caves have beautiful carvings that illustrate the life of Lord Buddha. Some of the caves have exquisite carvings and sculptures and have been based on the classical Indian art. Then, you have the Kailash Temple in cave number 16, deemed to be the largest monolith structure in the entire world. Tourists come from far and wide to visit this amazing cave temple. Out of the numerous Buddhist Caves at Ellora, cave number 10, cave number 11 and cave number 12 are considered to be the most significant ones. Cave number 10 is a splendid example of Chaitya architecture in India.

It is named after Vishwakarma, the presiding deity of all architects. Cave number 11 is known as Do Tal. It is a three-story structure dating back to the 8th century AD. Cave number 12, known by the name of Teen Tal, is also a wonderful three-story cave.

Bhaja Caves

The Bhaja Caves come under the Aurangabad district of Maharashtra. They are situated at a distance of approximately 12 km from Lonavla. It is believed that Bhaja caves date back to the 2nd century, i.e. to the rule of Mauryans in India, in the early Theravadin phase of Buddhism. There are eighteen caves in to and each other of them is adorned with magnificently chiseled images of Lord Buddha with different postures.

Along with that, there are also some representations of Buddha, in symbolic terms.

Also embellishing the Bhaja caves are the images of some animals and situations of some of the Buddhist tales. The twelfth

cave, also the biggest one, comprises of a prayer hall and boasts of splendid ancient Buddhist architecture. In the last cave is a 'Dancing couple' structure, a must see attraction of Bhaja. One of the oldest caves in India, Bhaja Caves comprises of a number of Viharas, which are mainly used as hostels for the Buddhist monks being taught there. Last but not the least, are the amazing stupas inside as well as outside the caves

Junnar Caves

Junnar caves are situated in the Aurangabad district of Maharashtra. They lie at a distance of approximately 177 km from the city of Mumbai, on the Mumbai-Aurangabad route. There are three major groups of caves in the hills surrounding Junnar plains, of which the most prominent ones are Tulija Lena and the Ganesh Lena. All of the Junnar caves, situated in India, were founded somewhere between 2nd Century BC and 3rd Century AD.

The first group of caves, the Tulija Lena, consists of the Chaitya hall, adorned with a circular dome ceiling. The second group is situated near the Manmodi hills is archaeologically quite significant. Archaeologists visit these caves on a frequent basis, to testify the sculptures and images in the caves. The third group of caves, known as Ganesh Lena, is approximately 4 km to the south of

Junnar. This group consists of a number of small cells and viharas, with most popular ones being the Chaitya Cave No. 6 and the Ganesh LenaVihara.

Kanheri Caves

Kanheri Caves are situated in the heart of the Sanjay Gandhi National Park, Maharashtra. They lie at a distance of approximately 10 km from Borivali, Mumbai. They are almost 109 in number and date back to somewhere between 1st century BC and 9th century AD. Kanheri Caves signify a golden beginning and the end of Buddhism in the northern India. Buddhist Monks as well as traders, who travelled for religious favours, used to make use of these caves on a frequent basis.

At the top of the caves stand exquisite sculptures of goddess Tara and Goddess Bhrukti. The central structure is that of Avalokiteswara, with five symbols, each in the right as well as the left. Another major attraction of Kanheri Caves is the Chaitya Cave, dating back to somewhere between 4th century AD and 5th century AD. Magnificent decorative woodwork embellishes the roof of this cave. The outer sides of the wall are adorned with sculptured statues of Buddha, mainly the Avalokiteswara incarnation.

These are Buddhist caves or monasteries where monks practiced their austerities around the first century AD. And unlike the artistic extravagance of Elephanta, they are spartan and bare. The complex contains more than a hundred tiny cells cut into the flank of a hill, each fitted with a stone plinth that evidently served as a bed. There is also a congregation hall supported by huge stone pillars that contains the dagoba, a kind of Buddhist shrine. And if you pick your way up the hill you will find channels and cisterns that are remnants of an ancient water system that channeled rainwater into huge urns. In fact, Kanheri is probably the only clue to the rise and fall of Buddhism in Western India.

Karla Caves

Karla Caves are situated in the state of Maharashtra, near the Pune-Mumbai Road. They lie at a distance of approximately 20 km from Lonavla and 40 km from Pune. The caves of Karla date back to the 2nd century BC and are known for their Chaitya Hall, intricate sculptures and pillars with ingenious architecture. Chaitya hall boasts of its amazing structural design. The rooftop is built of teakwood and even the pillars have been beautifully carved. One of the pillars of Karla Caves, with four lions at the top, now forms the national emblem of India. A number of sculptures cut out of rock, based on numerous animals as well as different forms of human life, adorn the caves of Karla. The other attractions include a stone stupa and 37 pillars, chiseled with the figures of prosperous men and women on elephants, prostrating before Lord Buddha. The bouncing sunshine falling inside the shrine further lends it a mystic as well as a tranquil aura.

Barbara Caves

Barbara Caves are situated in Barbara Hills, at a distance of approximately 20-25 km to the north of Gaya, Bihar. These hills are famous for the four rock cut caves that are sited here. Dating back to the 200 BC, these caves were constructed during the reign of Emperor Ashoka, for the Ajivikas. Carved out of a huge granite rock, these caves look as if they are cut with a laser. The caves were designed in a way that they look like wood. Out of the four caves, the most significant one is the Lomas Rishi Cave. The facade of the cave has been based on the architecture of the thatched huts, which used to house ascetics in the ancient period. The interiors of the cave consist of a big rectangular chamber, adorned with amazing glass-like polish. The nearby Nagarjuni Hill also consists of two caves, namely Sudama and Chaupar. Founded by Asoka's grandson, these caves boast of polished interiors, but plain exteriors.

Indasala Cave

Indasala Cave is situated near Rajgir in the state of Bihar. It lies at the base of a sharp cliff, halfway up the side of Giriyek Mountain. On the top of the mountain stands the Hansa Stupa. The Hansa Stupa holds the distinction of being the most complete stupa in India, till date. Hiuen Tsang, the famous Chinese traveller also visited this stupa. The stupa as well as the story behind its construction finds a mention in the accounts of his travels in India.

The Indasala Cave is an important Buddhist pilgrim destination in India, as it served as the venue of one of the most thoughtful discourses given by Lord Buddha, known as the Sakkapanha Sutra. Also, a number of verses of Dhammapada, namely 206, 207 and 208, were given by Buddha here only. The Indasala Caves also served as the residence of Buddhasrijnana, the famous commentator on the Guhyasamaja Tantra, for some time.

6
Places Associated with Buddhism–Rock Edicts

Rock Edicts

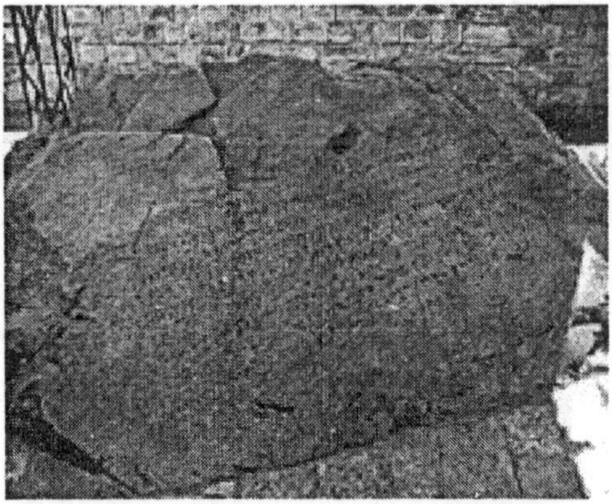

Ashoka was one of the greatest emperors of India. His high ideals and philosophies are inscribed in the form of rock edicts all over northern India. The Ashokan rock edicts are basically a collection of 33 inscriptions that are carved on the Pillars of Ashoka along with big boulders, caves, etc. These rock edicts have not been modified in any way and are preserved the way they were carved originally.

The rock edicts of India are found in many places of northern India as well as Pakistan. These rock edicts are supposed to be one of the primary concrete evidences of the spread of Buddhism. The inscriptions on these edicts basically provide information about the spread of Buddhism in India and other places. Ashoka was a great follower of Buddhism and these edicts support his effort to spread Budhha's word in different places of his sovereign. According to the information provided by the rock edicts of Ashoka Buddhism spreaded as far as Mediterranean as well as Srilanka outside his monarch. Many Buddhist monuments and temples were constructed during this period in order to promote this peaceful religion and make the world aware of Lord Buddha's teaching and philosophy. The rock edicts declare emperor Ashoka's faith in the concept of Dharma or Righteousness.

The inscriptions focus on not just the religious aspects and practices but more on the social and moral concepts. The rock edicts very clearly mention the efforts of Emperor Ashoka to spread Buddhism throughout the kingdom. However, the rock edicts do not mention the Four Noble Truths or the Eight Fold Path to Nirvana. This could be because Ashoka wanted to remain simple in his approach to Buddhism and connect with the common man.

The rock edicts describe Ashoka as the "Beloved of Gods". This was discovered in an inscription that was discovered in the year 1915 on a rock edict. The language used in the rock edicts and inscriptions of Ashoka was Pali. As the edicts and inscriptions were scattered over different parts of the empire, as many as four scripts were used in different edicts and inscriptions of Ashoka. These scripts were Kharoshti, Greek, Aramic and Brahmi.

Ashoka describes himself in the rock edicts as 'Beloved of Gods' and 'King Priya-darshi'. An inscription discovered in the year 1915 on a rock edict confirmed the identification of king Priya-Darshi with Ashoka. The language used in these edicts is mainly Pali. But they are also written in different other languages as they were spread through a vast region. As for example the inscriptions found on the eastern part of India were written in Magadhi Language, using the 'Brahmi' script. In the western part of India the language used is closer to Sanskrit, which used the 'Kharoshthi' script. The edict 13 was written in Greek language and the other bilingual edict written in Greek and Aramaic. The Major Rock Edict of Ashoka is found out of the town of Junagadh on the Saurashtra peninsula in the state of Gujrat in India. The edict is high up on a large, domed mass of black.

Granite stone on Girnar hills. The difficulty in climbing the hills allows only few Jain monks or pilgrims to visit the edict. This neatly etched rock edict is inscribed with Brahmi' script. The different places where Ashoka's Rock Edicts were found are- Allahabad-Kosam, Bairat, Barabar hill caves, Broach, Brhmagiri,Delhi-Meerut, Dhauli, Gavimath. Girnar, Gujjara, Jatinga-Rameshwar, Jaugada, Kalsi, andanar, Lampaya, Lauriya-Araraj, Lauriya-Nandangarh, Mahasthan, Mansehra, Maski, Nigali-Sagar, Palkigundu, Pataliputra, Rajula-Mandagiri, Rampurya, Rummindei, Rupanath, Sahasram, Sanchi, Sarnath, Shahbazgarhi, Siddapur, Sohgaura, Sopara, Suvarnagiri, Tamralipti, Taxila,Ujjain, Yerragudi.

The locations of the edicts are of geographical importance, as the selection of their sites was not arbitrary. They were deliberately placed either near habitations, or on important travel routes, or at places of religious interest, thereby ensuring that they would be available to as many people as possible. The reasons for the choice of a particular site will be given in this appendix. Such an analysis demands considerable archaeological evidence to substantiate literary and epigraphical indications. Unfortunately not all the sites have as yet been excavated. Therefore, in some cases the reasons can only be regarded as suggestions. Concerning the importance of the sites in south India we must keep in mind that the area within which most of the edicts have been found tallies closely with the gold-mining area of the south. The *Arthasastra* mentions this activity in the south, and speaks of gold as a special commodity of trade with the south. Thus this region was of tremendous economic importance and this may have been the prime reason for the selection of some of the southern sites. The inscriptions were probably situated in the well-inhabited mining areas or along the main routes to this area. The list of sites is given in alphabetical order.

Ahraura

The site lies 23 miles south of present day Banaras. It was probably on the route from Magadba to the west coast, as were Sabasr Amand Rupanath.

Allahabad-Kosam

(Pillar Edicts I-VI, the Queen's Edict, and the Kausambi Edict or Schism Edict). The importance of Allahabad, the old Prayaga was largely due to its being a pilgrim centre. It lay on what was then a great sandy plain between the two rivers, the Ganges and the Yamuna Hsuan Tsang describes it as a place sacred to Hindus and relates many legends regarding its temples. Since the Kausambi Edict is directed to the *mahamattas* of Kausambi, this pillar was originally situated at the latter site. The site is the same as modern Kosam on the left bank of the Yamuna, twenty-eight miles south-west of Allahabad. Kausambi having been a place of religious importance in Buddhist times may well have attracted pilgrims from various parts of the country and would therefore have been an excellent site for the edicts. The Asokan pillar was inscribed on, at later period by various rulers including Samudragupta and Jahangir. It would appear from Samudragupta's inscription that the pillar was still at Kausambi during the Gupta period. Probably Jahangir was responsible for its removal to the fort at Allahabad, which he did in imitation of Firoz Shah, who had brought similar pillars from Topra and Meerut to Delhi. Both Allahabad and Kausambi being on the river Yamuna, the transportation of the pillar would not have been too difficult.

Bairat

(Minor Rock Edict and the Bbabra Edict). Bairat is located in Rajasthan, forty-two miles north-east of Jaipur. It has been identified with Viratathe capital of the Matsya state. The presence of the Bhabra Edict addressed specifically to the *Sangha* is explained by the fact that the remains of two monasteries have been discovered on a hill about a mile south-west of Bairat. More recently, excavations in the region revealed a brick chamber resembling a *stupa*. It may have been an early Buddhist shrine of a period prior to the emergence of the *stupa* as a regular Buddhist feature. This points to Bairat being an old and established centre of Buddhism. It was thus both a centre of religious activity and an important city of the region, with a large population.

Barabar Hill Caves

The inscriptions in these caves are donatory, and therefore their significance does not rest in the particular importance of their site. The caves were in a group of hills girdling the city of Rajagrha.

Broach

Broach is not mentioned in the edicts nor is it the site of any Asokan inscription, but from other evidence it was clearly the most important commercial centre for trade with the West and as such must have held a prominent position during the Mauryan period. It is mentioned with great frequency in the Periplus. Since the ports of Saurastra had communication with the cities in the Ganges basin they became important in the course of this trade. Furthermore the Aparanta area to the west of the Mauryan empire had considerable Greek and Persian contacts, which no doubt the people of this area wished to maintain.

Brahmagiri

(Minor Rock Inscription). Excavations at the site have revealed considerable archaeological evidence pointing to Brahmagiri having been an important centre in south India even well before the Mauryan period. Continual habitation for many hundreds of years resulted in its emerging as an influential town, particularly after it had become one of the southern outposts of the Mauryan Empire. It may also have been the starting point of pilgrimages to the sources of the two rivers, Godavari and Kaveri.

Delhi-Meerut and Delhi-Topra

(Pillar Edict, I-VI and I-VII respectively). The Delhi-Meerut and the Delhi-Topra pillars are so called because they were transported to Delhi by Firoz Shah from their original sites at Meerut and Topra. Both these places lie to the north-west of Delhi. Neither of these two sites has been excavated as yet so that the reason for their being selected as the location for the Pillar Edicts remains uncertain. It would appear that both sites were important stopping places on the road from Pataliputra to the north-west. If there were caravanserals at these two points no doubt a fairly large habitation must have grown up around them.

Dhauli

Rock Edict of Ashoka at Dhauli

(Major Rock Edicts). The Dhauli inscription has been cut high on a rock in a group of hills which rise abruptly from the surrounding plain. The site has been identified with Tosali which is mentioned by Ptolemy as a metropolis. It was situated near the sacred pool of Kosala-Ganga and thus developed into a religious centre as well. The identification of Dhauli with Tosali is most convincing and is borne out by the text of the 1st Separate Edict. which is addressed to the mahamattas of Tosali.

It seems reasonable that the edicts would be as near the city as possible if not actually within it.

Gavimath

(Minor Rock Edict). Gavimath is situated in modem Mysore and is one among the group of places in the neighbourhood of Siddapur where this edict is found with great frequency. Its importance may have been largely due to its being a mining area or on an important route.

Girnar

(Major Rock Edicts). The importance of Gimar is not difficult to account for. It is situated one mile to the east of Junagarh in Kathiawar. That it was a site of immense importance is amply proved by the number of major inscriptions to be found there,

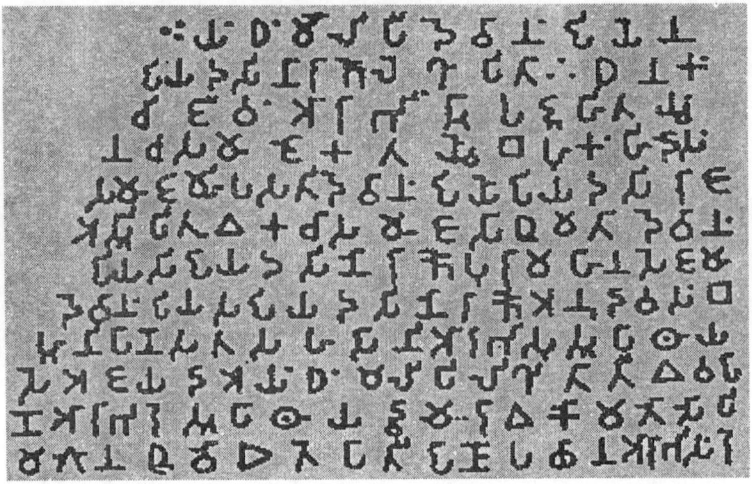

Ashoka's First Rock Inscription at Girnar

including apart from those of Asoka, those of Rudradaman and Skandagupta. It is mentioned as Girinagar in the Brhat Samhita. By tradition the mountain is regarded as sacred both to Brahmans and Jainas.

Its importance was increased by the fact that during the reign of Candragupta a dam was constructed on the Sudarsanalake in the neighbourhood of Girnar. The Rudradaman inscription informs us that the lake was originally built by Pusyagupta the provincial governor of Candragupta. Subsequently conduits were worked from it by Tusaspa in the reign of Asoka. It refers to the town of Girinagar in the vicinity. It appears from the inscription of Skandagupta that the lake continued to supply water to the surrounding area until well into the Gupta period, eight hundred years later. Since it was the source of water for irrigation it must have been the focal point in the area. It is possible that in the Asokan period the city of Girnar was closer to the lake than is the present site of Junagadh, since it would have been more practical to build the city as near the water supply as possible. Thus the hill on which the inscription was engraved was the centre of considerable activity.

7

Places Associated with Buddhism–Monasteries

The term Monastery has been derived from a Greek word 'monasterion', which means the habitat and workplace of a community of monks or nuns. In Buddhism, a monastery is known as Vihara or Gompa. The exact time of the emergence of Buddhist monasteries is not known. It is believed that they emerged somewhere around the fourth century BC. The practice of vassa, the retreat undertaken by Buddhist monks and nuns during the South Asian rainy season, is said to have been the inspiration behind the Buddhist monastery.

Under Vassa, wandering Buddhist monks and nuns were confined in a particular place for the monsoon season, lasting for approximately three months. This was done to prevent them from upsetting new plant growth or becoming stranded in stormy weather. These retreats were organized in the pavilions and parks donated to the sangha, by wealthy supporters. With the passage of time, this routine of staying in the retreats during the vassa retreat advanced into an austere lifestyle for the nuns and the monks.

They started living in the monasteries as a Sangha, throughout the year. Initially, Buddhist monasteries were used as residence by the Sangha, as a whole. However, later this practice changed in some of the counties and only the monks started residing in the monasteries. For the nuns, nunneries started coming up. In the Indian subcontinent, Buddhist monasteries progressively grew into centers of learning. They served as the places where philosophical principles were developed and debated. In some of the countries, monasteries also became large landowners.

Peasant families worked on the land of the monastery and in exchange, gave the monks a portion of their yearly crop. While in others, the monastery came under the ownership of a single monk, who passed it on from generation to generation. In the Theravada traditions of Southeast Asia and Sri Lanka, one can also find forest monasteries. Theses monasteries do not perform scholarship or ceremonial duties. Rather, they are devoted to the study of Buddhist meditation.

A Buddhist monastery is meant to be the main center for worship, isolated meditation and religion teaching. Monasteries are also one of the major attractions of the tourists visiting the beautiful.

Bomdila Monastery

Bomdila Monastery

Bomdila Monastery, situated in state of Arunachal Pradesh, dates back to the year 1965. It owes its inception to the 12th reincarnate of Tsona Gontse Rinpoche, who got this monastery built before his death in the year 1966. The monastery of Bomdila is an imitation of the Tsona Gontse Monastery, located at Tsona in South

Tibet. The main prayer hall of the monastery was added later on by the 13th reincarnate of Tsona Gontse Rinpoche.

This hall was later sanctified by His Holiness, the 14th Dalai Lama, in October 1997. Apart from the prayer hall, Bomdila Monastery also comprises of a temple of Lord Buddha and residential quarters for the monks. Also known as Gentse Gaden Rabgyel Lling Monastery, it is one of the most important centers of the Lamaistic faith of Mahayana Buddhism.

Tawang Monastery

Tawang Monastery is situated in the state of Arunachal Pradesh. It lies at a distance of approximately 180 km from Bomdilla. The monastery stands hovering on a hilltop, at an altitude of approximately 10,000 ft. One of the largest Buddhist monasteries in India, Tawang Gompa also holds the distinction of being the birthplace of the 6th Dalai Lama. Known by the name of Galden Namgyal Lhatse also, the monastery dates back to the year 1860-61. Founded by Merak Lama Lodre Gyamtso, it is an epitome of Buddhist architecture and belongs to Gelukpa sect. One of the major attractions of Tawang Monastery is the huge gilded statue of Lord Buddha. It also houses a rich collection of invaluable manuscripts, books and thankas (depicting Lord Buddha as well as other tutelary deities in diverse poses). At the entrance of the monastery is a pond, known as Dung Gyur Mani. The monastery sources its water from this pond only. The entry gate, kakaling, as well as the ceiling stand adorned with a range of exotic paintings. The assembly hall, Dukhang, is beautifully decorated with silver caskets and thankas, mainly of Goddess Sri Devi. The entire complex of the monastery is spread over an area of 135 sq. m. The complex comprises of 65 residential buildings and 10 other structures. There is also a library, housing old scriptures (mainly Kanjur and Tanjur numbering 850 bundles).

Dhankar Gompa

Dhankar Gompa is a Buddhist monastery situated in the Spiti Valley of India. It stands perched at a height of 12,774 feet and falls between the towns of Kaza and Tabo. Dhankar was the erstwhile capital of Spiti Valley Kingdom during the 17th century.

The monastery was built approximately one thousand years ago. One of the major attractions of Dhankar Monastery is statue of Vairochana (Dhayan Buddha), consisting of 4 figures seated back to back. It also houses a collection of various crumbling thankas.

Situated around 1 km away Dhankar Gompa is the small village of Shichilling, which houses the new Dhankar Monastery. The new monastery belongs to the Gelugkpa School of Order and serves as the residence of approximately 150 monks. To the south of the gompa is a national park, where you might get to see the snow leopard.

Tabo Monastery

Tabo Monastery is situated in the Spiti Valley of Himachal Pradesh. Perched at an altitude of 3050 m, it offers magnificent views of the valley below. The monastery was founded by the great scholar, Richen Zangpo, in the year 960 AD. Tabo Gompa, located in India, was meant to serve as an institution for advanced learning. Infact, it saw tremendous growth in the Tibetan art between 11th century and 20th century. Tabo Monastery is adorned with a number of exquisite ancient murals, some of them dating back to the 11th century.

The entire complex of the monastery consists of nine structures, out of which the most popular one is the Duwang Lakhang. The huge Chaitya Hall boasts of magnificent architecture as well as a few splendid Buddhist sculptures. Apart from these, there is the four-faced magnificent Buddha idol, the Amitay Buddha (in seated position), a stucco idol of Bodhisattva Maitreya, etc. Because of its beautiful murals and stucco images, Tabo has been given the name of 'The Ajanta of the Himalayas'. The monastery serves as the residence of approximately sixty monks. The main shrine inside the monastery is that of Tsug Lhakang and it is situated at the heart of the complex. Tabo Monastery also has a rich collection of clay statues of the Buddha, painted in the Kashmiri style.

Enchey Monastery

Enchey Monastery is situated in Gangtok, the capital of Sikkim. The monastery is approximately two hundred years old and follows the Nyingma Order. The name 'Enchey Monastery' means 'the Solitary temple'. The monastery was built with the intention that no other construction would be allowed near it.

It is believed that the monastery was built on the site blessed by Lama Drupthob Karpo, a tantric master famous for his power of flying. It is also said that the Lama built a small hermitage at the site of the monastery, after he came here from Maenam Hill in South Sikkim.

The shape of a Chinese Pagoda was given to the monastery during the reign of Sikyong Tulku (1909-1910). The Enchey Gompa of India also serves as the residence of approximately 90 monks, belonging to the Nyingma order. The monastery houses splendid images of Gods, Goddesses and a number of religious objects. Every year a puja is held at the monastery, on the 18th and 19th day of the 12th month of the lunar calendar. Sacred dances are also performed at this time. January is the time for "Chaam" or religious masked dances at the monastery.

Pemayangtse Monastery

Pemayangtse Monastery is situated in the Pemayangtse town of Sikkim, India. It lies at a distance of approximately 140 km to the west of Gangtok. Perched at an altitude of 6840 ft, it is one of the oldest monasteries of Sikkim. Lama Lhatsun Chempo got the monastery built, mainly for the 'ta-sang' lamas (the purest of monks). However, with time, the monastery started serving the entire community.

Pemayangtse Gompa of India boasts of a splendid collection of ancient Buddhist antique idols, scriptures as well as sculptures. Magnificent sculptures and gracefully decorated paintings adorn the first floor of the monastery. One of the major attractions of the Pemayangtse Monastery is a seven-tiered painted wooden structure, portraying Guru Rimpoche's Heavenly Palace 'Santopalri'. Late Dungzin Rimpoche took five years to finish this structure single handedly. Presently, it is situated on the top floor of the monastery. The Chaam (monk dance) is held every year, on the 28th and 29th day of the 12th month of the Tibetan Lunar Calendar. The lamas also take part in the dance and dress up in beautiful costumes, to represent Mahakala and Guru Drag-dmar. The dance comes to an end, on the third day, with the unfurling of the Ghyo-Ku' and gigantic embroidered Buddhist scroll.

Phensang Monastery

Phensang Monastery is situated in Gangtok, the capital of Sikkim, on the gentle slope that spreads from Kabi to Phodong. This monastery dates back to the year 1721, the time of Jigme Pawo. It belongs to Nyingmapa Order and serves as the residence of approximately three hundred monks belonging to the same order.

However, the journey of the monastery from the 18th century to the present times has not been totally pleasurable. In 1957, Phensang Gompa of India witnessed a devastating fire that engulfed it entirely. However, the lamas of the monastery put in efforts to build it again. In 1948, their hard work paid off and the monastery got completed. Phensang hosts an annual festival on the 28th and 29th day of the tenth month of the Tibetan Calendar (usually December). Sacred dances are performed at this festival, which takes place two days before the Sikkimese New Year.

Phodong Monastery

Phodong Monastery is situated in the northern part of the state of Sikkim. It lies at a distance of approximately 28 km from the capital city of Gangtok. One of the six most important monasteries of Sikkim, Phodong dates back to the early 18th century. However, the monastery that we see today is not the original one and was rebuilt.

Presently, it boasts of being one of the most beautiful monasteries in the state and serves as the residence of approximately 260 monks. The monastery also has a rich collection of some ancient murals. The annual festival at Phodang Gompa of India takes place on the 28th and 29th day of the tenth month of the Tibetan Calendar (usually December).

The celebrations of the festival include the performance of religious dances by the monks.

Ralang Monastery

Ralang Monastery is situated in the southern part of Sikkim. It lies at a distance of approximately 6 km from Ravangla. There is a story attached to the construction of the monastery. After the fourth Chogyal came back from his pilgrimage, the Karmapa performed the Rabney (blessing). As per the ceremony, he threw grains from the Tsurphu Monastery in Tibet (the main seat of Karmapa).

The ground where the grains fell, eventually, became the site for the Ralang Monastery. The monastery belongs to the Kagyupa order. One of the most significant as well as the most blessed monasteries in Sikkim, Ralang also serves as the residence of approximately one hundred monks. The period of 1975-1981 saw reconstruction work being carried out in the monastery. Then, in 1995, a new monastery, known as Palchen Choeling Monastic Institute", was built. Constructed by the 12th Gyaltsab Rimpoche, the monastery still retains the genuine Tibetan architecture. One of the major attractions of the Ralang Gompa of India is its amazing collection of paintings. Ralang monastery plays host to an annual festival, known as Pang Lhabsol or the worship of Mount Khangchendzonga and Kagyad. Chaam masked dances are also organized every year, on the 15th day of the seventh month of the Buddhist calendar (August-September) and on the 29th day of the tenth month of the Buddhist calendar (December). The sacred Mahakala Dance takes place every year in the month of November.

Rumtek Monastery

Rumtek Monastery is situated in the state of Sikkim, India. It lies at a distance of approximately 24 km from the capital city of Gangtok. It serves as the seat of His holiness Gyawla Karmapa the XVI, the head of the Karma Kagyu order of Tibetan Buddhism.When the 16th Karmapa came to Sikkim, Rumtek Monastery, then Dharma Chakra Centre, was in ruins.

He got the monastery rebuilt and it got completed after four years, in 1966. Rumtek Gompa of India is almost a replica of the original Kagyu headquarters in Tibet.

Perched at a height of 5800 ft, it comprises of the main shrine-temple, the monastery, a retreat center, a monastic college (Shedra), a nun's hostel, some stupas, a protectors shrine and other establishments for the community, along with a number of other religious institutions. Every year, a dance festival is held here, on the 28th day and 29th day of the 10th month of the lunar calendar.

Tashiding Monastery

Tashiding Monastery is situated in the state of Sikkim. It lies at a distance of approximately 40 km from Gyalshing and 19 km to the south east of Yoksum. Perched on top of the hill rising between the Rathong River and the Rangit River, it provides breathtaking views of the scenery below.

Tashiding Gompa of India dates back to the year 1717, which coincided with reign of the third Chogyal Chakdor Namgyal. It is located on the site blessed by the great Guru Padmasambhava.

The legend associated with the monastery goes that Padmasambhava shot an arrow into the air to select the place where he would sit in meditation. The place where the arrow landed, eventually, became the site of the Tashiding Monastery. Built by Ngadak Sempa Chembo (one of the three wise men who consecrated ceremony of the first lama), Tashiding Monastery belongs to the Nyingmapa order. The main temple of the monastery was rebuilt some time back only. It stands encircled by traditional buildings, chortens and mani (stone plates).Mani stand inscribed with the sacred Buddhist inscriptions, like "Om Mane Padme Hum". The stone plates are the work of the master craftsman, Yanchong Lodil. The chortens, preserving the relics of Sikkim Choygal and lamas, stand at the far end of the complex. Out of the numerous chortens, the most significant one is the 'Thong-Wa-rang-Dol'. Literally meaning 'Saviours by mere sight', this chorten is believed to cleanse the soul of any person who looks at it.The annual festival of the monastery, known as the

Bumchu Ceremony, is held in 14th and 15th day of the first month of the Tibetan Calendar. The ceremony, which is held at midnight, attracts devotees from far and wide.

Namgyal Tsemo Gompa

Namgyal Tsemo Gompa was founded in the early 15th century, around the year 1430. It stands atop the crag behind Leh palace, having a full view of the town of Leh. And because of this position, it offers some of the most splendid visuals of the town. The Namgyal Tsemo Gompa of Ladakh was founded by King Tashi Namgyal and has been named after him only. It boasts of a rich collection of some ancient manuscripts and wall paintings.

One of the most treasured possessions of the monastery is a three-story high solid gold idol of Maitrieya Buddha (future Buddha, also known as the laughing Buddha). Namgyal Tsemo Monastery of Leh Ladakh also houses a statue of Avaloketesvara and Manjushri, approximately one story high. Near the monastery is an old fort, which, because of neglect, lies mostly in ruins now. Also in the vicinity, are a number of associated temples. These temples remain open only during morning and evening. When the temples open up, a monk from the Sankar Gompa comes to attend to the butter-lamps in front of the images.

Monasteries of Ladakh

A Buddhist monastery is meant to be the main center for worship, isolated meditation and religion teaching. Monasteries are also one of the major attractions of the tourists visiting the beautiful valley of Ladakh. People come to Ladakh either to enjoy its scenic beauty or visit its monasteries or both. The entire valley of Ladakh is dotted with monasteries of all kinds, belonging to various orders or schools of Buddhism. Almost all these monasteries are sited at scenic locales, enhancing their magnificence further.

Also, they boast of a rich collection of Buddhist relics like thankas, murals, sculptures, scriptures, etc. Typically, the monasteries in Ladakh have been located at isolated areas, away from the hustle bustle of the routine life. This lends an air of peace and tranquility to them. In this section, we have provided information about almost each and every Buddhist monastery of Leh Ladakh, India. More specifically, we have covered the following monasteries of Ladakh...

Alchi Gompa

Alchi Gompa dates back to the year 1000 AD and was built by the Translator, Rinchen Zangpo. He even made a reference about the monastery in his biographies. It is written that he brought thirty-two sculptors and wood carvers from Kashmir, for the construction of the Alchi Monastery of Leh Ladakh. The monastery is sited at a distance of approximately 67 km to the west of Leh. One can easily see an Indian touch in this monastery, especially in the way its paintings have been made. Three sacred temples, with the main one being that of Rinchen Lhakhang at Lotsa Lhakhang, make up a major part of the Alchi Gompa of Ladakh. However, there are other temples also, namely Jamyang Lhakhang (Manjusri temple), Sumtsag Lhakhang and so on. There are a number of images inside the monastery. However, the main one is that of Vairocana. The other images include the ones of the five Buddha Families, along with their attendant deities.

Bardan Monastery

Bardan Monastery of Ladakh, standing atop a rocky crag, lies at a distance of approximately 12 km to the south of Padum. It belongs to the Dugpa-Kargyud monastic order. Infact, it was one of the first centers of Dugpa-Kargyud monastic order to be set up in Zanskar. Bardan Gompa of Leh Ladakh dates back to the 17th century. A number of smaller monasteries in the region come under the management of Bardan. One such monastery is the Sani Gompa. Bardan Gompa consists of a large Dukhang, assembly hall. All the other structures within the monastery are structured around the Dukhang only. The hall boasts of some of the most magnificent statues of Buddhist divinities, along with some small stupas in clay, bronze, wood and copper. Near Bardan

Monastery lies the monastery of Muney, famous for its splendid art treasures.

Chemrey Gompa

Chemrey Gompa of Ladakh was founded by Lama Tagsang Raschen and dates back to the 17th century. Situated at a distance of approximately 40 km to the east of the town of Leh, this monastery belongs to the Drugpa Order. Infact, it serves as the residence of approximately 20 monks of the diminishing Drugpa community, and also their young apprentices. Chemrey Monastery of Leh Ladakh was initially built to serve as a memorial to King Sengge Namgyal. There are a number of shrines situated inside the monastery.

However, one of the major attractions of the Chemrey Gompa is the one-story high image of Padmasambhava it houses. Other than that, the monastery also boasts of a precious collection of scriptures, having title pages in silver and the text in gold letters. The successive reincarnations of Lama Tagsang Raschen have being serving as the incumbents of the Chemrey Gompa of Ladakh, since quite a long time. The monastery also serves as the venue for the festival of sacred dances. The festival takes place, on an annual basis, on the 28th and 29th day of the 9th month of the Tibetan calendar. The dances, at this annual festival, are performed in association with the festival of an initiatory ritual.

Diskit and Hundur Gompa

Both the Diskit Gompa as well as the Hundur Gompa are situated in the Nubra Valley of the Ladakh region. Situated quite near the monasteries, at a slightly higher altitude, is Lachung Temple. One of the oldest temples of this area, the temple has a huge idol of Tsong-kha-pa, crowned with a Gelugpa yellow hat. Hundur Monastery of Leh Ladakh is situated just below the main road, near the bridge and Diskit Monastery is situated nearby.The Diskit Gompa of Leh Ladakh dates back to the 14th century and owes its inception to Changzem Tserab Zangpo, a disciple of Tsong-kha-pa. At the heart of Diskit Monastery is an elevated cupola, which stands adorned with a beautiful fresco that illustrates the Tashilhunpo Gompa of Tibet. There are a number of shrines inside the monastery's complex, like Kangyu-lang, Tsangyu-lang, etc. Also, hundreds of Mongolian and Tibetan texts have found their storehouse inside these temples.

Diskit Gompa has quite an interesting legend attached to it. It is believed that a Mongol demon once lived here and was considered to be a sworn enemy of Buddhism. He was annihilated near the monastery. However, even after his death, his body kept coming back to the monastery again and again. It is said that even today the wrinkled head and hand of the demon lie inside a temple of the monastery, which is filled with fierce Gods and Goddesses.

Hemis Monastery

Hemis Monastery holds the distinction of being the biggest as well as the wealthiest monastery of Ladakh. It dates back to the year 1630 and was founded by the first incarnation of Stagsang Raspa Nawang Gyatso. Hemis Monastery is positioned inside a gorge, at a distance of approximately 47 km from Leh. Belonging to the Dugpa Order, it stands on the western bank of the Indus River.

The monastery also boasts of a very rich collection of ancient relics. The array of items kept inside the monastery consist of a copper-gilt statue of the Lord Buddha, various gold and silver stupas, sacred thankas and several other exquisite objects. Situated slightly higher than the Hemis Gompa of Leh Ladakh, is a sacred hermitage, founded by Gyalwa Kotsang. The meditation cave of Gyalwa, along with his footprints and handprints on the rock and sacred shrines, still bring back his memories to life.The Hemis Monastery also serves as the venue of an annual festival, known as the Hemis Festival. This festival is celebrated as a commemoration of the birth anniversary of Guru Padmasambhav. On the day of the Hemis Festival, the thangka of the monastery is displayed, with a gap of twelve years between successive displays. The Thanka is the sacred appliqué-work tapestry wrought with pearls, which depicts Guru Padmasambhava. And not to be forgotten is a sacred mask dance that is performed at the monastery every year. The dance takes place on 9th and 10th day of the fifth month of the Tibetan calendar.

Karcha Monastery

The Karsha Monastery of Ladakh is situated in the Karsha village of the Zanskar region. The full name of Karsha, the largest monastery of Zanskar, is Karsha Chamspaling. Phagspa Shesrab, the translator of Zanskar first founded this monastery. The monastery, as it stands today, was the result of the efforts of the Teacher, Dorje Shesrab. It was under him only that the monastery flourished and prospered. Shesrab Zangpo of Stod was the one to introduce the Gelukpa Order in the Karsha Gompa of Leh Ladakh.The monastery consists of a number of shrines and boasts of some of the most exquisite wall paintings, by the Lama Dzadpa Dorje. The collection of Karcha Gompa also includes the bone relics of Dorje Rinchen. It serves as the residence of approximately 100 monks. The Gustor Festival is celebrated at Karsha every year, on the 28th and 29th day of the sixth month of the Tibetan calendar. The celebrations also include the performance of the sacred dance. Temples built by Rinchen Zangpo, the translator, known as the Thugsjechhenpoi Lhakhang and the Lhakhang Karpo, are situated near the Karsha Monastery. Also close by are the monasteries of Khagsar, Purang and Phagspa and a nunnery called Dorjezong, situated at the top of the valley.

Lamayuru Monastery

Lamayuru Monastery is situated in Ladakh, in between Bodhkharbu and Kha-la-che, on a steep rock mountain. It lies at a distance of approximately 127 km to the west of Leh town. Lamayuru Monastery belongs to the Red-Hat sect of Buddhism and houses approximately 150 Buddhist monks. The monastery is made up of a number of shrines and also has a very rich collection of thankas and magnificent wall paintings. At the outset, the Lamayuru Monastery consisted of five buildings, out of which only the central one exists today.

Every year the Lamayuru Gompa plays host a masked dance, which takes place on the 17th and 18th day of the 5th month of Tibetan lunar calendar. The monks from the monasteries of the nearby areas also come to take part in the celebrations. There is an interesting legend associated with the Lamayuru Gompa of Leh Ladakh. It is said that the Lamayuru Valley used to be a clear lake, at the time of Sakyamuni (the Historical Buddha). And, nags (holy serpents) used to reside in the lake. Bodhisattva Madhyantaka had once a prediction quite a long time back that the lake would eventually be dried, making way for the construction of a Buddhist monastery. The legend moves further to state that Mahasiddhacharya Naropa, an 11th century Indian Buddhist scholar, sat in meditation for a number of years in one of the caves in Dukhang. He was the one who caused a crack in the hillside surrounding the lake. Through this crack, the lake started draining. When the lake dried out, the scholar found a dead lion lying inside it. On the same spot, where he found the tiger, he constructed the first temple of the area, known as the Singhe Ghang (Lion Mound). Another legend has it that the building of Lamayuru Monastery was constructed, as per the instructions of King of Ladakh, under the direction of Rinchen Zangpo, the Translator. After this, the monastery came under the administration of the Zhwa-mar-pa (Red Hats). Later, Dharmaraja Jamyang Namgial offered the monastery to Chosje Danma. And this led to the observance of the rituals of the Digung Kargyud School, with the monastery being renamed as Yungdrung Tharpaling. Today, the Lamayuru Monastery is served by the successive reincarnations of Skyabsje Toldan Rinpoche.

Likir Gompa

The name Likir means "The Naga - Encircled". The reason behind this naming of Likir Gompa of Ladakh is that it stands surrounded by the bodies of the two great serpent spirits, the Naga-rajas, Nanda and Taksako. The monastery is situated at a distance of approximately 62 km to the west of Leh town. Lhachen Gyalpo, the fifth king of Ladakh, offered the site where the monastery now stands, to Lama Duwang Chosje. The Lama, a great champion of meditation, blessed the site offered to him, after which the construction on the monastery was undertaken.

The Likkir Monastery of Leh Ladakh was founded in the later half of the 11th century, around the year 1605. It belongs to the Yellow Hat Sect, founded by Tsongkhapa. It consists of a number of shrines inside its complex. Presently, it serves as the residence of approximately 120 Buddhist monks. The monastery also has a school, in which almost thirty students study. In the 15th century, Likir Gompa came under the influence of Lodos Sangphu. A disciple of Khasdubje, he made efforts to see that the monastery flourished and prospered. From that time onwards and till today, the monastery continues to be under the Tsongkhapa order. The ritual of the three basic Pratimoksa disciplines, the basic Buddhist teachings, are observed at the Likir Monastery, even in the present times. The Gompa also serves as the venue of an annual event Dosmochey, the assembly of votive offerings. This event takes place from 27th day to 29th day of the 12th month of the Tibetan calendar. During Dosmochey, sacred dances are also performed at the monastery. The Likir Gompa Ladakh has been served by the succeeding reincarnations of Naris Rinpoche, since quite a long time and continues to do so. The monastery also houses a protective deity, which stands inside, wearing a golden armor. There are two Dukhangs (assembly halls) inside the monastery, one of them relatively new. The older one is on the right of the central courtyard of the monastery and comprises of six rows of seats for the lamas. Inside this Dukhang are the statues of Bodhisattva (Lord of All He Surveys), Amitabha (Buddha of the West), Sakyamuni (the Historical Buddha), Maitreya (the Future Buddha or Buddha of Compassion) and Tsong-kha-pa (Founder of the yellow-hat sect). After you exit from this Dukhang, you will see the new Dukhang, diagonally across from the courtyard's entrance. The main image in the new Dukhang is that of Avalokitesvara, with 1000 arms and 11 heads.

Mashro Gompa

Mashro Gompa of Ladakh is located on the opposite bank of the Indus River across the Thiksey Monastery. It dates back to the first part of the 16th century. The Mashro Monastery of Leh Ladakh boasts of an amazing compilation of an array of ancient and very beautiful thankas, of which some are even in the form of 'mandalas'. The monastery also serves as the venue for a festival of oracles, which takes place on an annual basis.

The festival, held in early March, is considered to be one of the important events in the religious calendar of the Ladakhis. In the preparation for the festivals, young monks are selected as oracles. These monks are required to go through meditation, fasting and ritual purification for a long period of time, to gain spiritual strength. At the time of the festival, they carry out amazing exploits with the help of swords and knives, cavorting blindfolded along narrow parapets.

Matho Gompa

Lama Dugpa Dorje founded the Matho Gompa of Ladakh in the 16th century. It is situated on the opposite bank of the River Indus, at a distance of approximately 26 km to the southeast of Leh town. Matho is the only gompa of Ladakh that belongs to the Saskya order of Tibetan Buddhism. The oracle of the monastery is a priest, who resides in the monastery itself. Also situated near the monastery, are a number of sacred shrines, of which one is dedicated to the guardian deities. Matho Monastery of Leh Ladakh hosts the Matho Nagrang Festival, on an annual basis. The festival takes place on the 14th and 15th day of the first month of the Tibetan calendar. All the monks participate in the sacred dances, performed at this annual event. It is believed that, during Matho Nagrang Festival, two gods, known as the Rongtsan, descend to visit the monastery. Matho Monastery also boasts of housing an amazingly rich collection of four hundred years old Thankas. On the right side of the monastery courtyard, is the entrance to the Dukhang (the main assembly hall). Paintings of the Guardians of the Four Directions adorn the verandah of the Dukhang. Inside are two rows of seats for the lamas, along with a throne seat that is reserved for the Rimpoche, the head lama of Matho. There are four statues behind the throne seat, that of the thousand-armed Avalokitesvara, Maitreya, Sakyamuni and a blessing Buddha. The entrance wall displays Mahakala, the fiercest Buddhist guardian divinity, on the left and other protecting deities, on the right.

Phyang Monastery

Phyang Monastery of Ladakh is situated at a distance of approximately 40 km to the west of the Leh town. It belongs to the Red Hat Sect of Buddhism. The site where the monastery now stands was once a part of the numerous monastic properties, offered during the time of Dharmaraja Jamyang Namgial to Chosje Damma Kunga. The hill of Phyang served as the venue of a monastery, known as Tashi Chozong, established in the year 1515. A monastic community was introduced to the monastery and with this started, the first establishment of the Digung teachings in Ladakh. The traditions of the Digung teachings began with Skyoba Jigsten Gonbo. In the present time, the Phyang Gompa of Leh Ladakh is under Apchi Choski Dolma. The monastery is served by the successive reincarnation of Skyabje Toldan Rinpoche. There are a number of sacred shrines situated inside the monastery complex. Also, there are some exquisite wall paintings, dating from the royal period, adorning the monastery. Another attraction of Phyang Gompa is its 900 years old museum. Its rich collection boasts of numerous idols, thankas, Chinese, Tibetan and Mongolian firearms and weapons, etc. The festival of Gang-Sngon Tsedup is held every year from 17th day to 19th day of the first month of the Tibetan calendar. The monastery also serves as the venue of the sacred dances, held every year on the 2nd and 3rd of the 6th month of the Tibetan calendar.

Phugtal Gompa

One of the most isolated monasteries of the region, the Phugtal Gompa of Ladakh dates back to the early 12th century. Situated in the Zanskar region, the Phugtal Monastery stands at the opening of a huge cave. The cave is located on the front of a huge gorge, which also serves as a passageway for a major tributary of the southern Lungnak River (Lingti-Tsarap). To reach the Pugthal

Monastery of Leh Ladakh, one can also go through the Padum-Manali trekking route. A number of chapels are situated inside the premises of the Phugthal Gompa. And one of these chapels even reflects a strong Indian touch. The frescoes as well as the ceiling decorations, adorning the chapel, bear the marks of artistic and iconographic influence of India. Also, the monastery serves as the residence for approximately 40 monks.

Rangdum Gompa

The Rangdum Gompa of Ladakh was founded in the 18th century. Situated in the Zanskar region of Ladakh, it serves as the residence of approximately 40 monks. The monastery rises over a centrally ascending mound, entrenched around by the bifurcated route of a mountain stream. The Rangdum Gompa of Ladakh gives the appearance of an age-old fortification, which is standing as the protector of a mystical mountain valley. One of the major attractions of the monastery is its small museum. It boasts of a rich collection of fascinating Tibetan as well as other relics. The Rangdum Monastery of Leh Ladakh owns the entire valley around it, comprising of the fields tilled by the villagers, the pastures, hills and even the streams. The villagers staying around the monastery are the descendents of the serf-tenants of the monastery and do not have any land of their own.

Rhizong Gompa

The Rizong Gompa of Ladakh was founded by the great Lama Tsultim Nima in the year 1831. It belongs to the Gelukpa Order, and is situated at a distance of approximately 73 km from the Leh town. The monastery serves as the residence of approximately 40 monks. However, they have to follow some very strict rules. The inmates of the monastery are not permitted to have anything on their person, except for religious robes and books. Rizdong Monastery of Leh Ladakh consists of a number of shrines inside its complex.

The gompa also has quite a rich collection of the painting blocks of Lama Tsultim Nima's biography as well as a number of objects made and books composed by the first Sras Rinpoche. Serving as the incumbents of the Rizdong Monastery, are the successive reincarnations of Lama Tsultim Nima and his son, Sras Rinpoche. A nunnery, known as Chulichan (Chomoling) is located near the monastery, at a distance of approximately 2 km. comprising of about 20 nuns, the nunnery is under the control of the governing body of Rizong Monastery only. The nun, known as Chomos, worship at the temples of the monastery itself. They also perform a number of chores for the monastery like spinning wool, milking, extracting oil for the temple lamps, etc.

Sani Monastery

Sani Monastery of Ladakh belongs to the southern branch of the Drukpa Kagyupa School. It is situated on the road to Kargil, at a distance of approximately 6 km to the west of Padum. The entire Sani Monastery of Ladakh has been built in parts, each dating back to a different century. The chorten inside the oldest part of Sani Monastery is believed to be erected in the 2nd century AD. On the other hand, the Dukhang (assembly hall) of the monastery is said to be constructed in the early 17th century. The monastery is built in the form of a castle and has the Kanika Stupa in the backyard of its walled complex. Because of the existence of this stupa, it is believed that the monastery was associated with Kanishka, Kushan ruler of 2nd century AD. The central praying hall is situated in the main building of the monastery and stands ornamented with a rich collection of the statues of popular Buddhist divinities and Kargud-pa high lamas. Even the walls of the praying hall are adorned with frescoes and thangkas.

As you exit the main building from the backside, you will come across a small, neglected chapel. Although not in a very good condition, still the chapel stands adorned with some of the most beautiful stucco murals depicting landscapes and floral designs, based on the life of Guru Padmasambhava. Outside the complex of the monastery is one of the eight most important cremation grounds of Tibetan Buddhists. The cemetery stands encircled by a ring of ancient rock-carvings, which reveal a touch of the Indian art.

The Sani Gompa of Leh Ladakh is also alleged to be connected with the famous Indian Yogi Naropa. It is believed that the Yogi meditated under the Kanika Stupa, situated in the backyard of the monastery. The same spot, where the Yogi sat in meditation, now houses a small room with a veiled bronze statue of the Yogi. Every year the statue is unveiled in late July, i.e. on the eve of the Naro-Nasjal Festival. In this festival, the lamas from Bardan Monastery perform masked dances as ritual offering.

Sankar Gompa

Sankar Gompa of Ladakh is located at a distance of approximately 3 km from the town of Leh. A subsidiary of the Spituk Gompa, it belongs to the Gelukpa or the Yellow Hat Sect. The monastery also serves as the official residence of the Ladakh's head of Gelukpa Sect, known as The Kushok Bakul. There are time restrictions for visiting the Sankar Monastery of Leh Ladakh. You can also go either between 7:00 am and 10:00 am, or between 5:00 pm and 7:00 pm. These restrictions have been placed because a few of the monks, of the yellow-hat sect, attached to the monastery reside here permanently. To the right of the front yard of the monastery is the Dukhang (assembly hall). Both the sides of its entrance are adorned with the paintings of the Guardian of the Four Directions. On the left wall of the entrance verandah is a "Wheel of Life", held by Yama. As you enter the Dukhang, you will come across some relatively new paintings of various Buddhas, along with guardian deities. There is also a throne inside the Dukhang, reserved for the head lama of the monastery. On the right-hand side of the throne is an image of Avalokitesvara (Lord of All He Surveys), with 1000 arms and 11 heads.

The central image inside the Sankar Monastery is that Tsong-kha-pa, founder of the yellow-hat sect of Buddhism, along with his two chief disciples. To the left of this image is another image of Avalokitesvara, again with 1,000 arms and 11 heads. And to its right is a case full of Tibetan bronzes. There are a number of other images also, like those of Sakyamuni (the Historical Buddha), The Present Buddha, Maitreya (the Future Buddha), White Guardian and Amchi (the Buddha of Medicine). Diagonally opposite to the door, leading to the small inner courtyard of the monastery, is Dukar Lokhang, a temple devoted to the deity Dukar. The main image inside Dukar Lokhang is that of Dukar, inset with turquoise and shown with 1,000 arms, 1,000 feet, 1,000heads, and 100,000 eyes. To the right of the image is a statue of Maitreya (the Buddha of the Future). Sankar Gompa also has the possession of Kandshur, the 108 volumes of Buddha's teachings.

Shanti Stupa

Shanti Stupa of Ladakh is located on the hilltop at Changspa. It can be reached quite easily from the Fort Road. The Stupa was constructed by a Japanese Buddhist organization, known as 'The Japanese for World Peace'. The aim behind the construction of the stupa was to commemorate 2500 years of Buddhism and to promote World Peace. His Holiness, the Dalai Lama inaugurated the Shanti Stupa in the year 1985. A magnificent white-domed structure, the Shanti Stupa of Leh Ladakh offers spectacular views of the sunrise and sunset. The stupa looks best at night, when it is beautifully illuminated with glittering lights. A large number of tourists come to Ladakh every year to visit this amazing stupa.

Shey Gompa

Shey Gompa of Ladakh is situated on a hillock, at a distance of approximately 15 km to the south of Leh town. The monastery was erected on the instructions of King Deldon Namgyal, in the memory of his late father, Singay Namgyal. The main image inside the Shey Monastery is that of Buddha Shalyamuni. It is a huge image of the seated Buddha and is considered to be the biggest metal statue and the second largest Buddha statue in the Ladakh region. Copper sheets, gilded with gold, make up this amazing Buddha statue.

The image also contains sacrificial offerings such as grain, jewels, holy signs and mantras inside it. On both the sidewalls of the Buddha statue, are displayed the 16 Arhats (Worthy Ones who have achieved Nirvana), eight being on each side. The back wall of the statue is painted with the images of the two chief disciples of Buddha, namely Sariputra and Maudgalyayana. There is hardly any wall around the Buddha statue that is not painted with any image. A large bowl of wax with a central flame, symbolizing divinity and purity, is placed in front of the Buddha statue. This flame burns continuously for one year, before getting replaced. Some exquisite murals adorn the second story of the Shey Monastery of Leh Ladakh. While, the lower story comprises of a large library and is decorated with murals depicting Buddha, with various types of hand gestures. An annual festival is also held at Shey Gompa, on the 30th day of the first month of the Tibetan calendar.

Spituk Gompa

Spituk Gompa of Ladakh dates back to the 11th century. It owes its inception to Od-de, the elder brother of Lha Lama Changchub Od. Od-de led to the establishment of a monastic community at this place. A three-chapel monastery, Spituk is located at a distance of approximately 8 km from the town of Leh. The name "Spituk", meaning exemplary, has been derived from a statement of a translator, Rinchen Zangpo, about the monastery. He said that an exemplary religious community would develop there, providing the name Spituk for the monastery. At that point of time, the Spitok Monastery of Leh Ladakh was under the Kadampa School. Slowly and gradually, as time passed, the monastery started functioning under Dharmaraja Takspa Bum-Lde Lama Lhawang Lotus. He brought about the restoration of Spituk and introduced the stainless order of Tsongkhapa (Gelukpa). Even today, the monastery functions under the Gelukpa order only. Three other monasteries of Ladakh, namely Stok, Sankar and Saboo, are considered to be the branches of Spituk Gompa. The incumbents serving in all these monasteries are the successive reincarnations of Skyabsje Bakula Rinpoche. The main image inside the Spitok Monastery is that of Lord Buddha. Along with that is a sacred image of Amitayus, about a finger high in length. Tsongkhapa, himself, presented this image, to Takspa Bum-Lde. It also boasts of a rich collection of thankas, ancient masks, antique arms, etc. And not to be missed is an impressive image of Mahakaal. The Dukhang (main temple) also has a high throne at its far end, reserved for the Dalai Lama. The door beside this central throne leads to dark old chapel. The central images inside the chapel are those of Tsong-kha-pa, his two chief disciples and of the Buddha. Spituk Gompa also plays the host to the Gustor Festival, held every year. The festival takes place from the 27th to 29th day in the eleventh month of the Tibetan calendar. A sacred dance also forms a part of the celebrations.

Stakna Gompa

Stakna Gompa of Ladakh is situated on the right bank of the Indus River, at a distance of approximately 25 km from the town of Leh. The name, 'Stakna' literally means 'tiger's nose'. The monastery was so named because it was built on a hill, which is shaped just like a tiger's nose. Stakna Monastery of Leh Ladakh owes its inception to Chosje Jamyang Palkar, the great scholar saint of Bhutan. It formed a part of the many religious estates offered by the Dharmaraja Jamyang Namgial to the saint, around 1580 AD. The central image inside the monastery is that of the sacred Arya Avalokitesvara from Kamrup (Assam). Stakna belongs to the Dugpa order and serves as the residence of approximately 30 monks. The successive reincarnations of the Stakna Tulku continue to serve as the incumbents of the monastery, preserving the teachings of the Dugpa order. Stakna Gompa also has a number of monasteries attached to it, namely Mud and Kharu and those of Stakrimo, Bardan and Sani in Zanskar.

On entering the central courtyard, one comes across the Dukhang (main assembly hall). The head lama got seven feet high, silver gilted chorten erected inside the Dukhang, in the 1950s. The chorten comprises of a statue of the Buddha as well as numerous Buddhist texts. The left wall of the Dukhang is adorned with three new paintings, those of the Tsephakmad (a Buddhist deity), Sakyamni (the Historical Buddha) and Amchi (the Medical Buddha). The wall opposite to the Dukhang entrance is also painted with three images, those of a Bodhisattva, Padma Sambhava (8th century Indian Buddhist scholar and translator of Buddhist texts into Tibetan) and Tshong-san-gompo (an early king of Tibet). To the right of the hall are the statues of Sakyamuni (Past Buddha), the Present Buddha and Maitreya (Future Buddha). And, the throne of the head lama of Stakna lies on the left side of the Dukhang.

Stok Gompa

Stok Gompa of Ladakh is situated at a distance of approximately 15 km to the south of the Leh town. It dates back to the 14th century and was founded by Lama Lhawang Lotus. Stok is a subsidiary of the Spituk Gompa and belongs to the yellow-hat sect of Buddhism. As you enter the verandah of the monastery, you will come across bright friezes, depicting the Guardians of the Four Directions. The Dukhang of the monastery was repainted, not a long time back, and displays a rich collection of banners and thankas.

The left-side wall is adorned with the images of Vajrapani (Vajra-in-Hand) and Avalokitesvara (Lord of All He Surveys), in his four-armed manifestation. At the same time, the right-side wall stands proud with the images of Sakyamuni (the Historical Buddha) and his two disciples, Amchi (the Buddha Medicine), Tara (the Saviouress) and Nangyalma. There are two thrones inside the Dukhang. The central one has been reserved for the Dalai Lama, while the one on its right is for the head lama of Stok Monastery.

As you exit the Dukhang from the backside, you will come across a small chapel. The chapel holds the distinction of being the oldest structure inside the Stok Monastery of Leh Ladakh. The central image inside the temple is that of Tsong-kha-pa, the founder of the yellow-hat sect of Tibetan Buddhism. There are also images of Avalokitesvara, in his four-armed manifestation, and Maityreya, the Future Buddha or Buddha of Compassion, inside the chapel. To the right of the Dukhang is another chapel. It boasts of an array of Buddha images, depicting the eight hand gestures of Buddha.

One of the major attractions of the Stok Monastery is its own library. The library has a complete set of the Kandshur, the 108 volumes of the Buddha's teachings. A new temple, dedicated to Avalokitesvara, was added to the monastery some time back. The central image inside the temple is that of Avalokitesvara, with his 1,000 arms and 11 heads. A ritual dance-mask takes place near the gompa, on the 9th and 10th day of the first month of the Tibetan calendar.

Stongde Monastery

Stongdey Monastery of Ladakh is considered to be the second largest monastic institution in the Zanskar region. It is situated on the road to Zangla, at a distance of approximately 18 km to the north of Padum. The Stongde Gompa of Leh Ladakh serves as the residence of approximately 60 monks. Founded in the year 1052 by Lama Lhodak Marpa Choski Lodos, the monastery comes under the Tsongkhapa Order. The incumbents serving at Stongdey are the successive reincarnations of Nari Tulku.

The main prosperity of the Stongdey Monastery came under the influence of Shakya Zangpo, of Stongdey itself. There are a number of beautiful temples situated inside the complex of the monastery. Another major attraction of the monastery consists of the gorgeous wall paintings adorning its interiors. Stongde also serves as the venue of Gustor festival, an annual festival that takes place on the 28th and 29th day in the eleventh month of the Tibetan calendar. On the day of the festival, the monks perform the sacred dance in the monastery.

Takthok Monastery

Takthok Monastery of Ladakh is situated in Sakti Village, at a distance of approximately 46 km from the town of Leh. The site where the monastery is now situated, once served as the meditation cave of Mahasidhas "Kunga Phuntsog". The name Takthok literally means 'rock-roof'. The monastery was so named, as both its roof as well as walls are made up of rock. Tak Thok belongs to the Nying-ma-pa sect of Buddhism, also known as the Old Order, and serves as the residence of approximately 55 lamas. It is the probably the only Gompa in Ladakh that follows this order. Every year a festival is held at the Tak Thok Gompa of Leh Ladakh, on the 9th and 10th day of the sixth month of the Tibetan calendar. Celebrations of the festival include sacred dances and the ceremony of hurling a votive offering. To the left of the central courtyard is the cave chapel of the monastery. Opposite the chapel are the images of Padme Sambhava and Avalokitesvara. There is a small cave behind these images, believed to the place where Padme Sambhava lived and meditated for three years. On the right of the central courtyard, lies the Dukhang or the main assembly hall. Murals of guardian divinities adorn the verandah entrance to the Dukhang. But, they are displayed only at the time of the annual festival of the monastery. There is a throne inside the Dukhang, reserved solely for the Dalai Lama. It is situated just opposite to the Dukhang entrance. The wall to the left of the throne stands decorated with the mural of Padmasambhava, while the one on the right has a painting of Sakyamuni. Also inside the Dukhang, are the statues of Maitreya (the Future Buddha or Buddha of Compassion), Padmasambhava and Dorje Takposal (a manifestation of Padmasambhava). Takthok Monastery also houses the Kandshur, the 108 volumes of Buddha's teachings.

Thiksey Gompa

Thiksey Gompa of Ladakh is situated at a distance of approximately 18 km from the town of Leh. One of the most beautiful monasteries of Ladakh, it belongs to the Gelukpa Order of Buddhism. Sherab Zangpo of Stod got the Thikse Monastery built for the first time, at Stakmo. However, later Spon Paldan Sherab, the nephew of Sherab Zangpo, reconstructed the monastery in the year 1430 AD. The new monastery was sited on a hilltop, to the north of Indus River. Thikse Monastery of Leh Ladakh houses a temple, known as Lakhang Nyerma. This temple, built by Rinchen Zangpo, the Translator, is dedicated to Goddess Dorje Chenmo. A huge temple in its time, today it stands mostly in ruins. Apart from this temple, there are a number of other sacred shrines inside the monastery complex. The monastery also has a rich collection of numerous valuable artifacts and ancient relics. Thiksey Gompa serves as the residence of approximately eighty monks. It has been served, for quite a long time, by the successive reincarnations of the Skyabsje Khanpo Rinpoche. The monastery also plays the host to Gustor ritual, organized from the 17th to 19th day of the ninth month of the Tibetan calendar. Sacred dances also form a part of this ritual, which takes place on an annual basis.

Zongkul Monastery

A cave monastery of Zanskar, Zongkul stands perched on the rock face of the Ating George. There is an interesting legend associated with the Zongkul Monastery of Ladakh. It is said to be connected with Naropa, the famous Indian Yogi from Vikramshila. In fact, it is believed that he even used the two caves of the monastery for the purpose of his solitary meditation. Even today, one can see Naropa's footprint embedded in the rock and his sacred spring, located inside the meditation cave. After Naropa meditated here, the monastery became the sacred place of meditation for all the mahasiddhas of Zanskar. Enlightened people like Dubchen Kunga Gyatso, Dubchen Nawang Tsering, Dzadpa Dorje, Karmapa, Kunga Choslag, etc. have used Zongkul for meditation purposes. The Zongkhul Gompa of Leh Ladakh consists of a number of blessed shrines.

It also boasts of a rich compilation of precious artifacts, like ivory image of Samvara, a crystal stupa, texts containing the spiritual songs and biographies composed by the successive mahasiddha, etc. Not to be missed are the splendid murals, made by Zhadpa Dorje almost 300 years ago.

8

Places Associated with Lord Buddha's Life

The presence of extensive Buddhist ruins distributed so widely across the whole of India is a remarkable phenomenon. Buddhism was a dynamic force that was born and thrived in India for 1700 years. Between the 5th century BC and 12th century A.D. the whole of India was rich with the culture of Buddhist life that spread to other parts of the world.

Lumbini

Lord Buddha was born in Lumbini, in the southwestern region of Nepal, almost 2500 years ago. Ever since then, the city has always continued to be the central point of Buddhism. Lumbini, in the present times is a small quiet town in the southwestern Terai plains of Nepal, where the ruins of the old city can still be observed.

Maya Devi Temple at Lumbini

The followers of both Hinyana and Mahayana sects of Buddhism worship Lumbini. The furbished up garden and the environs of Lumbini have the remnants of many of the ancient Stupas and monasteries. A large stone pillar is said to be set up by the Mauryan emperor Ashoka in 250 BC which bears a message about the birth of Gautama Buddha.

The Tourist Attractions in Lumbini are several and the beauty and charm of Lumbini promises to arouse interest in all kinds of tourists. The most important attraction of Lumbini is the holy temple of Maya Devi. The temple has a stone sculpture of Maya Devi in labor pain. The image shows her holding the branch of a tree while Buddha is getting birth. The temple is very popular among the women having some or other fertility problem. Another variety of the same plant is known as Banyan; the same tree under which Buddha got enlightened. The Bo plantation and a newly planted forest close by provide an air of serenity to the surrounding. Lumbini is recently being modernized under the Master Plan of the Lumbini Development Trust, a non-governmental organization devoted to the re-establishment of Lumbini and its development as a pilgrimage spot.

Apart from its religious and historical importance, Lumbini offers cultural insights into the village life of south west of Nepal. The must see occasion is the weekly communal Bazaar. Villagers come from far distant places to buy grains, spices, pottery, jewellery, saris and various other items.

Bodhgaya

The city of Bodhgaya, located in the state of Bihar, 14 km south of Gaya; is the most famous Buddhist pilgrimage center in the world. The region around Bodhgaya formed the part of the first small kingdoms of India in the 7th century BC. It is the place where Gautam Buddha entered into meditation after being moved by the sufferings of mankind. After gaining Enlightenment, Gautam became Buddha and spread his message of love and peace to the whole world.

To mark the spot where Gautam Buddha had attained Enlightenment, the great Mauryan ruler King Ashoka built a small

shrine here in the 3rd century BC. After that the subsequent rulers left their mark on this shrine, which finally took the shape of the Mahabodhi temple that is still there. In 528 BC Prince Siddhartha Gautama came here in search of truth. However the actual association and the facts about the place have always eluded us. Bodhgaya is the place where the wandering prince Siddhartha sat in meditation below a Bodhi Tree (Peepul tree). It is also famous for its Mahabodhi Temple and is reckoned as the most important Buddhist pilgrimage centre. His three days of initial meditation and subsequent seven weeks of enlightenment have been closely associated with various places in Bodh Gaya.

History remembers Bodh Gaya as Bodhimanda and the main monastery as the Bodhimanda-vihra (Pali). Being one of the four most important sites related to the life of Gautama (Kushinagar, Lumbini, and Sarnath complete the quadrate). The present city is a historians', tourists' and religious minded people's delight and is replete with numerous places and monuments that have a direct bond with the Enlightened Prince. The area remained the hotbed for Buddhism upto the 13th century till it was conquered by the Turks.

The city complete with the pilgrimage sites is beautifully situated on the shores of the broad but shallow Lilanjan River (also known as Neranjara). After crossing Bodh Gaya, the river joins Mohana River and forms Phalgu River which is considered sacred. Amongst the hustle of the city also stand proudly, the shrines dedicated to the Buddha by various countries like China, Japan, Bangladesh, Vietnam etc. The river surrounding hills and caves and the history of the city itself make it a must visit place for any nature and peace lover.

Bodh Gaya is the birthplace of Buddhism. Buddhists from all over the world are drawn to Bodh Gaya in the state of Bihar. This is the place where Lord Buddha gained enlightenment over 2,500 years ago and founded the religion based on compassion, reason and universal truths, shorn of ritual and superstition.

The Bodhi tree, under which he is said to have found the answers he was seeking after a long and hard meditation, is the core of the Mahabodhi Mahavihara Temple Complex, now a World Heritage site. The Mahabodhi temple has Jataka stories engraved on its walls.

Surrounding the complex are monasteries built by various Buddhist countries, in their own architectural styles. Several Buddhists temples and monasteries have been built by the people from China, Nepal, Sri Lanka, Myanmar, Bhutan, Vietnam, Tibet, Japan and Thailand around the Mahabodhi Mahavihara Temple complex. The Chinese temple has a 200 year old statue of Buddha. The Japanese and Burmese temple is shaped like a pagoda and the Thai Temple has a fantastic bronze state of the Buddha.

About 80 km from Bodh Gaya is Rajgir; there are remains of places associated with the Buddha such as the Gridhrakuta Hill, where he delivered sermons, or Venuvan, the tranquil bamboo grove near the hot springs he used to frequent.

Kushinagar

Kushinagar in Uttar Pradesh in India is the city of beautiful Stupas and Temples and considered to be one of the Holy Places in India. From Buddhist followers to the Indian devotees, this is one of the major pilgrimage destinations in Uttar Pradesh. Referred to as the Kushinara in ancient period, the city is a storehouse of architectural marvels. Archaeological excavations have unearthed a number of temples and Stupas which belonged to medieval India. Kushinara earlier was a part of the Malla kingdom and its popularity spread all over because of Lord Buddha. It is believed that Lord Buddha attained his salvation or the Mahaparnirvana in Kushinagar. One of the archaeological sites, the Tourist Attractions in Kushinagar will reveal a lot more about the art, culture and historical facts during Lord Buddha's period. The archaeologists and historians have unearthed important historical monuments in Kushinagar. Amongst the Tourist Attractions in Kushinagar, Uttar Pradesh one can get to see different things. From the beautifully designed Muktabandhana Stupa in Uttar Pradesh where the last remains of Lord Buddha were kept to the beautiful stone sculptures of Lord Buddha, the Tourist Attractions in Kushinagar, Uttar Pradesh are interesting and attracts tourists from all over. The stone figure of Lord Buddha was restored in 413-455 A.D. by King Haribala.

There are a number of tourist attractions in Kushinagar which you can explore during your Tours to Kushinagar. One of the major Tourist Attractions in Kushinagar which is also one of the important tourist places in Kushinagar is the Ramabhar Stupa.

Reclining Buddha at Kushinagar

One of the sacred shrines of Buddhists this is the place where Lord Buddha attained Mahaparnirvana. During Buddha Purnima a number of travellers India come to Kushinagar to take part in the festivities of Kushinagar.

Another major tourist attraction is the Nirvana Temple. Near this temple Lord Buddha passed away. There is a tall statue of Lord Buddha in this temple in Kushinagar. The Mathakaut Temple in Kushinagar is also one of the important tourist places in Uttar Pradesh. It is in this place, the archaeologists discovered a black stone image of Lord Buddha which was called the 'Bhumi Sparsha Mudra'. The last sermon of Lord Buddha was delivered over here. The Watt Thai Temple is one of the most visited temples in Kushinagar. The Japanese temple is also one of the beautiful temples in Uttar Pradesh and one of the major pilgrimage sites in Uttar Pradesh for the disciples. The Chinese temple with Oriental design and décor will also attract the tourists.

Sarnath

Sarnath derives its name from Saranganatha (Lord of the Deer). After the Buddha attained enlightenment in Bodh Gaya, he came to Sarnath. Here in the Deer Park, he delivered his first sermon or set in motion the Wheel of Law (Maha Dharmachakra Pravartan).

Buddhist Temple at Sarnath

On the day before his death, the Buddha named Sarnath along with Lumbini, Bodh Gaya and Kushinagar as the four places that his followers should consider sacred. The Emperor Ashoka, who spread Lord Buddha's message of love and compassion throughout his vast empire, visited Sarnath around 234 BC and constructed a stupa here.

Several Buddhist structures were built at Sarnath between the 3rd century BC and the 11th century AD and today this place has the most expansive ruins among the places related to the Buddha.

Explorations during a recent Japanese-funded UNESCO project have yielded this "biggest Buddhist settlement in all of Central India." The remains point to monasteries of enormous proportions. Earlier, eight structures had been identified. Now, 14 more monasteries and 23 stupas have been found. The Archaeological Museum here as well as the Chinese and Tibetan Temples are all worth a visit. Believed to have been built in 500

AD, the Dhamekh stupa, the largest in the region, marks the spot where the Buddha proclaimed his faith in front of his first five followers. The lower portion of this tall cylindrical stupa has fine floral carvings. It houses a stone slab with Buddhist inscriptions on it dating back to the 6th century BC. The sprawling green lawns around it provide the right environment to meditating monks.

The main excavation site is a vast expanse of low lying structures and standing amidst them one can view the various facets of Buddhist history, its interesting twists and turns, the rise and fall of empires and kingdoms. One can witness the ancient relics of Buddhist art, which was designed to communicate the message of the Buddha through signs and symbols. The earliest and most important relic is found in the Ashoka pillar that was erected in 250 BC. Four lions representing the spirit of India sit back to back with a wheel between them. The original piece is in the Sarnath archaeological museum.

As one explores the open complex of ruins, one can find monasteries dating back to different periods, reflecting different tenets of Buddhism. Kumar Devi was a Buddhist queen of Kannauj, who built perhaps the last of the great monasteries. Remnants of its basement and halls are visible here.

The dilapidated remains of the Choukhandi Stupa belonging to the Gupta period are a reminder that this is the place where the Buddha was reunited with his five disciples, who had previously deserted him. Standing on a terraced rectangular plinth, the Stupa is capped by an incongruous octagonal Mughal tower built by Emperor Akbar to commemorate his father's visit to the place.

The Mulagandha Kuti Vihar was built in 1931 by the Mahabodhi Society. The entrance of the vihar is dominated by a huge bell, a gift from Japan, and the interior contains a beautiful life-size golden image of the Buddha and colorful murals and frescoes painted by a Japanese artist.

The Sarnath Archeological Museum houses the superb Lion capital of the Ashokan Pillar. This symbol has been adopted as the national emblem of modern India.

Buddhists from various countries have built temples, each one unique in that it is built according to the architectural style of the country. Life in each of these temples-Chinese, Thai, Korean, Tibetan, Vietnamese, Sikkimese, or Burmese-revolves around cleaning the temple, meditating, reading holy books, teaching and offering food to the hungry and help to the needy.

The last monastery constructed before the Muslim invasion, the Dharmachakra-jina Vihara, was the largest of all. Kumaradevi, queen of King Govindachandra, who ruled in Benares from 1114-1154, built the monastery. There is a surviving fragment of stone inscription here, which records that in 1058, a monk presented a gift copy of the Prajna-paramita Sutra to the monastery. This incident provides the evidence of Mahayana activity at that time. The discovery of ancient statues of Heruka and Arya Tara in this area shows that Vajrayana was also practiced there.

Formerly, two great stupas adorned the site. However, today only the Dhamekha remains, assigned by its inscription to the sixth century. The Dharmarajika stupa built by Ashoka was pulled down in the eighteenth century by Jagat Singh, who consigned the casket of relics contained within it to the Ganges River. Huen Tsang described that Ashoka's pillar, which stood in front of the stupa, was so highly polished that it constantly reflected the statue of Buddha.

Deer Park was also the location of Shakyamuni's deeds in His previous lives. Huien Tsang mentioned a number of stupas near the monastery, commemorating these lives. One of stupas honors the event when bodhisattva offered himself as the deer. There was another observing the event when, as a six-tusked elephant, He offered his tusks to a deceitful hunter. The third stupa memorialized the event where He bodhisattva had been a bird, with Maudgalyayana and Sariputra as a monkey and an elephant. Today, the actual site of the Buddha's teaching at Sarnath as well as the several ruins in the area stand, enclosed in a park. Nearby, a well-planned museum houses a number of unearthed statues, many of them barely damaged, along with several other findings from the site. The museum's entrance is dominated by the famous lion capital from Ashoka's pillar. Adjacent to the park, is the

Mahabodhi Society's Mulaghandaluti Temple, an imposing building containing certain relics of the Buddha. Close by is the Society's sangharama and a library, which houses a rare collection of Buddhist literature. Also in the vicinity, are Burmese, Chinese and Tibetan temples. There is also a Tibetan monastery and the Institute of Higher Tibetan Studies nearby, where two hundred young monks practice and study the many aspects of the Buddha's teaching, to qualify for the degree of an Acharya. There is also a Tibetan printing press, The Pleasure of Elegant Sayings, which, over the last decade, has published more than thirty Tibetan texts of Buddhist treatises, otherwise hard to find. The wheel of Dharma that Shakyamuni first turned at Sarnath continues to revolve even today.

Other Buddhist Sites

Amravati

Amravati Stupa

The city of Amravati is situated in the state of Andhra Pradesh. It lies on the right bank of River Krishna, at a distance of approximately 65 km from Vijayawada. The erstwhile capital of Satavahana dynasty, it came under the influence of Buddhism through the Kushanas of Mathura. One of the major attractions of Amravati consists of the remains of a 2000-year-old Buddhist settlement,along with the great Buddhist stupa.

There is also a temple dedicated to Lord Amaresvara in the city. The Great *Stupa* of Amravati was constructed approximately

2000 years ago and stands taller than the stupa at Sanchi. Founded by an emissary of the great Emperor Ashoka, it is also known as the Mahastupa and Deepaladinne (the Mound of Lamps). The stupa is made of brick with a circular vedika and depicts Lord Buddha in a human form, subduing an elephant. It is adorned with 95 ft high platforms, protruding in four cardinal directions. Presently, Amravati stupa has been kept at the Government Museum of Chennai.

Nagarjunakonda

Nagarjunakonda is a valley situated in Guntur District of Andhra Pradesh. It lies at a distance of approximately 150 km from the capital city of Hyderabad. Nagarjuna Konda is named after Nagarjuna, a Buddhist monk, who lived here around the turn of the 2nd century AD. A magnificent example of ancient Buddhist architecture, it is remake of the original Buddhist site. The original valley was shifted, as it was at the danger of being submerged under the Nagarjuna Sagar Dam. The valley symbolizes a lost civilization, which flourished thousand years ago.

A number of excavations were carried out here, coming up with the Maha Chaitya, Viharas and Monasteries. Some of the most ancient items of Buddhism were also unearthed during the excavations, like Buddha statues, relics, stone images, Jataka tales encrypted panels and other items of Buddhist origin. It is believed that the antique sculptures belong to the Ikshvaku rule. The ruins of a university have also been found at Nagarjunakonda. There is also a museum, known as Nagarjunakonda Museum, housing all the important excavated items.

Champanagar

Champanagar is situated in the Bhagalpur district of Bihar, India. It lies at a distance of approximately 220 km away from the capital city of Patna. The significance of this place stems from the fact that it had the fortuity of being visited by Lord Buddha a number of times. Also, it served as the venue of a number of sermons delivered by Lord Buddha himself. He conveyed the Kandaraka Sutta (from The Middle Length Discourses), the Sonadanda Sutta (from The

Long Discourses) and numerous other significant discourses at Champanagar.

The place derives its name from the numerous Champaka trees that have been planted here. One of the attractions of Champanagar is a tank, known as Gaggara's Lotus Lake, popular for the splendid lotuses that grow there. On the banks of the lake is a huge plantation of Champaka trees, which used to be the most favored spot of Lord Buddha. To the left of the lake is a large water body, known as Sarovana Talab. A number of Buddha statues were found in 1900s, when the lake was cleaned.

Don

Don is situated in the state of Bihar. There is a legend associated with Don. It is believed that after the cremation of the mortal remains of Lord Buddha, an argument ensued between his four disciples over the division of his ashes. All of them agreed to hand over the task of division to a Brahmin, known as Dona. The Brahmin distributed the ashes in a very equitable manner. The disciples were so content with his distribution that they presented him with the vessel in which the ashes had been stored.

The Brahmin built a stupa to enshrine the holy vessel. Known as Dona's stupa, it has been presently reduced to a grassy mound. Over this mound is built a Hindu temple, where the statue of Tara, carved in the 9th century AD, is worshipped as a Hindu goddess. The entire episode relating to the distribution of the ashes as well as the presentation of the vessel is mentioned in the end of the Mahaparinibbana Sutra. Dona's Stupa was also visited by Hiuen Tsang, the Chinese traveler, and is mentioned in his account of travels in India.

Ghosrawan

Ghosrawan is a small village situated in the state of Bihar, India. The significance of Ghosrawan stems from the fact that it stands on the site of a very large and important Buddhist Monastery.

The monastery, probably known as the Kapotaka Vihara, even founds a mention in the account of travels of Hiuen Tsang, the famous Chinese traveller. One of the major attractions of

Ghosrawan is a huge statue of Lord Buddha, approximately 10 ft high.

The statue is located besides the lake, in the outskirts of the village. Carved out of shiny black stone, the statue presents a splendid sight. Situated near Ghosrawan is Tetrawan, another small village. This village has a temple, housing a rich as well as valuable collection of carved Buddhas and Bodhisattvas. Also nearby, is Nawada, boasting of a museum with an amazing display of Buddha statues found in the adjoining areas.

Gurpa

Gurpa is a small village, situated in the state of Bihar. It lies at a distance of approximately 33 km from Gaya, a Buddhist pilgrim destination in India. The village is considered as significant because of its association with Maha Kassapa, the successor of Lord Buddha.It is believed that Maha Kassapa was on his way to Kukkutapadagiri, his favourite hill resort. However, enroute he realized that his life was drawing to its end.

Throughout the way, rocks kept on hampering his progression. With his staff, he made the rocks open up and give him way. The moment he reached the top of the mountain, the rocks threw apart. He went inside the opening and fell into a deep meditative trance and the rocks closed around him. The legend in Buddhism goes that when Maitreya (the future Buddha) comes into this world, he will go to Kukkutapadagiri. There, he will wake up Maha Kassapa and receive Buddha's robe from him. Only after this, will he start announcing the new dispensation. This sacred mountain of Kukkutapadagiri is now called Gurpa. A few Hindu and Buddhist shrines and antiquities are located at the top, near the cave.

Hajipur

Hajipur is a small village situated in the state of Bihar. It lies at a distance of approximately 10 km from the capital city of Patna. In the ancient time, it was known as Ukkacala and was the first village to come after crossing River Ganga at Patna. The village of Hajipur gained significance, as it was the venue of one of the discourses given by Lord Buddha. Buddha preached the Cula Goplalaka

Sutta, a Middle Length Discourse, here. Along with that, it also houses some of the ashes of Ananda, the closest disciple and personnel attendant of Lord Buddha.

There is a legend associated with the Hajipur village in India. It is believed that Ananda, after realizing that his end was drawing near, decide to move towards the north of Rajgir town. As soon as King Ajatashatru came to know about this, he went after Ananda, escorted by his entire staff. Soon the news of Ananda's arrival reached the people of Vaishali and they started gathering at the banks of the River Ganga to welcome him. By the time King Ajatashatru caught up with Ananda, he was already in the middle of the river.

People of Vaishali, from one bank, and King Ajatashatru, from the other, started requesting him to come over to their side. In order to avoid disappointment and possible conflict, Ananda rose into the air and disappeared into a ball of flames. His ashes fell on both the banks of the river. On either bank, a stupa was built at the same spot where the ashes fell. With the river changing its course over time, the stupa on the southern bank got washed away. Even the one on the northern bank is now a grassy mound. Over this mound a Hindu temple has been built, known as Ramchaura Mandir.

Jethian

Jethian is a small village situated near Rajgir town of Bihar, India. In the ancient time, it used to be known as Lativana, or the Palm Grove. In 7th century AD Jethian also served as the seat of influence of Jayasena, the famous saint. Even Hiuen Tsang, the famous Chinese traveller, spent two years of his stay in India here, studying as a disciple Jayasena. Apart from that, it was in Jethian that Lord Buddha met King Bimbisara for the first time. Infact, there is a small story behind the meeting of Lord Buddha and King Bimbisara.

It is said that after coming from Sarnath and Bodhgaya, Lord Buddha left for Rajgir, in order to meet King Bimbasara. As soon as the King came to know of this, he went to the outskirts of the city, along with his entire staff, to welcome Him. There are numerous Buddhist structures as well as Buddha statues in and around Jethian. As you move towards this village, you will come across a large mound with a tank. The mound is believed to be the remains of the stupa built over the Supatittha Cetiya, the place where Lord Buddha stayed, when he was in Jethian.

Beside the mound, is a huge and impressive statue of Lord Buddha. Then, there are the statues of Padmapani and Buddha, situated very close to the mound. Not to be missed is the Chandu Hill, located at a distance of approximately 3 km from Jethian. This hill is quite popular as it houses the large cave of Rajpind (the cave mentioned in the Tripitaka).

Kesaria Stupa

Kesaria Stupa is situated in the Champaran (east) district of Bihar. It lies at a distance of approximately 110 km from the capital city of Patna. The Kesaria Stupa holds the distinction of being the largest in the world, standing at a height of 104 ft. The Archaeological Survey of India (ASI) excavated the stupa in the year 1998. It is believed to date back to somewhere around 200 AD and 750 AD has a circumference of almost 1400 ft. The amazing stupa serves as a splendid example of Buddhist architecture and archaeological preservation. The initial height of Kesaria Stupa, during the flourishing days of Buddhism in India, was approximately 150 ft. By 1934, when a massive earthquake shook India, the height of the stupa got abridged to 123 ft. After the earthquake, it further sank in the ground and got reduced to its present height. Interesting tales are attached with Kesaria. It is believed that Lord Buddha spent a night at this place before his Nirvana and gave his begging -bowl to the Lichhivis. It is further said that he even asked them to go back to Vaishali after his death. Lichhivis are alleged to have built this stupa, as a commemoration of the end-life of Lord Buddha. A six-floors structure, Kesaria Stupa stands as a reminder to the last days of Lord Buddha and his humanitarian approach towards people, independent of caste and creed. The excavations carried out at the site of the stupa have led to some noteworthy findings, like Islamic coins, arrow heads, copper and terracotta items, earthen lamps, decorated bricks etc. There are also a number of

Lord Buddha images, in "Bhoomi Sparsh Mudra" and other sitting postures.

Kurkihar

Kurkihar is a small village situated in the state of Bihar. It lies at a distance of approximately 22 km from the Gaya district. This large mound over which this village lies consists of the remains of a very old Buddhist Monastery. The village also boasts of two Hindu and is quite famous for a rich collection of Buddha statues and Bodhisattvas. Approximately 148 bronze artifacts were excavated from this area around the year 1930.

The excavated items consisted of Buddhas and Bodhisattvas in all shapes and sizes, bells, stupas and a number of rituals objects. All the items that were unearthed exhibit the highest degree of workmanship. A sizeable number of items, excavated over the years, have been kept in one of the Hindus temples of the Kurkihar village in India. Amongst all the relics, the most splendid one is the statue of Akshobhya Buddha, placed just outside the entrance of the temple.

The temple is also adorned with fourteen calved pillars, which date back to the 9th century. Some of the antiquities excavated from Kurkihar have been put up on display in the Patna Museum, while some others are in the Indian Museum in Calcutta.

Lauriya Nandangarh

Lauriya Nandangarh is situated in the state of Bihar. It lies at a distance of approximately 22 km from the district of Bettiah. Lauriya Nandangarh boasts of housing the Ashokan pillar, comprising of the six Ashokan Edicts. As per the version of the historians as well as the archaeologists, as many as forty pillars were built here by Emperor Ashoka. However, today only one pillar exists in complete form, at its initial location in Lauriya Nandangarh. The height of the pillar is more than twelve meters.

Even after so many years, the Mauryan polish used on the pillar still retains its radiance and shine. The pillar is carved with six Ashokan edicts, issued by the Emperor in the year 244 BC. The top of the pillar is adorned with a lion, in a squatting position. The face of the lion is distorted, as it received a cannon shot in 1660 AD. One of the major attractions of Lauriya Nandangarh is a large stupa, considered to be the one of the biggest stupas in India. The massive stupa is 24 m in height and has a circumference of almost 457 m.

Nalanda

Excavated Ruins of Nalanda Maha Vihar-2

Nalanda is situated in the state of Bihar. Founded in the 5th century AD, it lies at a distance of approximately 90 km from the capital city of Patna. Nalanda had the honor of being visited by Lord Buddha a number of times, in His lifetime. Even Hieun Tsang, the famous Chinese Traveler, stayed in this village for approximately 12 years, in the 7th century AD.

Nalanda came to be recognized as a famous center of Buddhist learning in India, only between 5th century and 12th century.

The university of Nalanda, apart from being the largest and oldest university of ancient time, was also first residential international university of the world. Around 2,000 teachers and 10,000 students, from all over the Buddhist world, stayed at this university. Emperor Ashoka and Harshavardhana got a number of temples, monasteries and viharas built here. Some time back, in 1951, an International Center for Buddhist Studies was set up at this place.

Excavated Ruins of Nalanda

Patna

Patna is the capital of the state of Bihar. It is situated on the banks of the holy river Ganga. In the ancient, the city was known by the name of Pataliputra. Patna has the fortuity of being visited by Lord Buddha, when he had to cross the mighty river on his last journey to Kushinagar.

It also serves as an entry point for most of the Buddhist destinations located in Bihar. Patna came under the empire of Ashoka, at the time of rise of Buddhism in India. Right from the advent of Buddhism in India, the city has been an important center of learning.

Patna also served as the venue of the Third Buddhist Council held under the patronage of Emperor Ashoka. One of the major attractions of the city, from Buddhism point of view, is the Patna Museum. The museum boasts of an amazing collection of Buddhist art, dating back to somewhere around 8th century AD to 12th century AD. The most magnificent pieces of art consist of the statues of Avalokitesvara and Maitreya. Apart from that, the city also houses some large pillars and the foundations of a Buddhist Monastery, known as Anand.

Pragbodhi

Pragbodhi Mountain is situated near Gaya district in the state of Bihar. The name Pragbodhi literally means 'Prior to Enlightenment'. The mountain derives its name from the sojourn of Prince Siddhartha here, before he received enlightenment.

He spent six years in rigorous practice of asceticism, after which he attained enlightenment. One of the places where he spent these six years came to be known by the Pragbodhi.

Today, the mountain has been renamed as Dhungeswara. As per the legends in Buddhism, Prince Siddhartha spent the time of his asceticism in a small cave half way up this mountain. The same spot now houses a small temple, looked after by Tibetan monks. A number of ancient stupas stand adorning the top of the Prag Bodhi Mountain of India.

Rajgir

Rajgir is situated in the state of Bihar, encircled by five holy hills. It lies at a distance of approximately 34 km from the city of Gaya. The name of the town has been derived from the words 'Raj Griha', meaning 'the abode of the king'. During the lifetime of Lord Buddha, Rajgir served as the capital city of the Magadh Empire.

It also has the distinction of serving as the host to Lord Buddha, during the reign of King Bimbisara. Prince Siddhartha (early name of Lord Buddha) came to Rajgir, after he renounced the luxuries of life and undertook asceticism. Two of the rock-cut caves of Rajgir were the favorite retreats of the Buddha. It was here that He preached two of his most renowned sermons.

Vaishali

Vaishali district is situated in the state of Bihar. It lies at a distance of approximately 60 km from the capital city of Patna. The place gains significance from the fact that it is here that Lord Buddha announced the imminence of his Mahaparinirvana. Vaishali also witnessed one of the eight great events in the life of Lord Buddha.

It was here that a monkey offered Him a bowl of honey. Lord Buddha also visited Vaishali five years after the attainment of His enlightenment. The Lichhvis offered a grand welcome to the Lord on his arrival in Vaishali.He displayed some extraordinary and divine presentations of his spiritual superiority here. This led to mass induction of people into Buddhism. Infact, it is believed that at that time around eighty four thousand people adopted Buddhism. One of the most important events that took place at Vaishali was the induction of females into the Sangha. It is believed that even Mahaprajapati Gautami, the foster mother of Buddha, joined the order here, along with the other Sakya-women.

Vikramsila

Vikramsila is a town situated in the state of Bihar, India. It lies at a distance of approximately 40 km from the city of Bhagalpur. One of the popular Buddhist destinations in India, Vikramshila cannot boast of a direct relation with Lord Buddha. It is mainly renowned for being one of the most significant centers of Tantric Buddhism, in the 8th century AD. It also houses the famous Vikramasila University, the main intellectual as well as learning center of Tantric Buddhism.

The University was built under the patronage of Dharmapala, a Pala king. Also known as Paramasaugata (meaning, the chief worshipper of the Buddha), he was a great follower of the Mahayana sect of Buddhism. The center of the university once had a huge temple, adorned with a life-size copy of the Mahabodhi tree. It is said that approximately 108 temples were constructed around it. Out of these, almost 53 temples were dedicated to the study of the Guhyasamaja Tantra. The entrance of the main temple stood guarded by two brilliant statues of Nagarjuna and Atisa Dipankar (a great scholar of the Vikramasila University). Vikramshila also lies very close to Champanagar, another famous Buddhist destination in Bihar.

Dhauli Hill

One of the important Buddhist destinations in India, Dhauli Hill is situated near Daya River, in the Khurda district of Orissa. It lies at a distance of approximately 8 km from the city of Bhubaneshwar. Dhauli hill holds the distinction of being the place where Emperor Ashoka renounced war and embraced Buddhism. The edicts of Ashoka, preserved here, serve as the perfect proof of the change of his heart. In his edicts, he has asked his administrators to govern with fairness and empathy. On the top of the rock edicts stands a chiseled elephant, the universal symbol of Lord Buddha.

Dhauli Hills, sited in India, also boast of a Shanti Stupa (the peace pagoda), situated on the opposite hill. Built through the Indo-Japanese collaboration, it has interesting legend attached to it. Japanese believe that almost seven centuries ago Mahatma Nichiren Imaha Bhikshu predicted that Fuji Guruji, the chief priest of Nipponzan Myohoji would come to India in 1930 from Mt. Minobu, the original holy place of the Nichiren sect. The prophecy came true, he came to India and got the Shanti Stupa built. A round edifice, the stupa is domed on top with mushroom-like structures. 'Speaking' stone panels, adorn the Shanti Stupa. The main stone panels comprise of the reclining Buddha, an elephant procession, the bodhi tree, footprints of Buddha bearing the chakra (wheel), a sleeping beauty fanned by female attendants, procession on horse back, and Emperor Ashoka renouncing war by offering his sword to Lord Buddha at Dhaulagiri Hill. The other major attractions of Dhauli Hill include Saddharma Vihar monastery, the ancient sculptures and the some very extraordinary art forms. Then, there are rock cut caves and a number of small Hindu temples, dating to the medieval age. Beautiful landscapes and scenic beauty of Dhauli further adds to its appeals.

Lalitagiri

The village of Lalitagiri is situated in the state of Orissa. It lies at a distance of approximately 90 km from the city of Bhubaneshwar. Lalitagiri dates back to the first century and is considered to be one of the earliest Buddhist establishments in the world. Even today, the ancient stupas, beautiful sculptures and the caves make the place look like that of an ancient age. The iconographical features of the Lalitagiri sculptures bear a strong resemblance to Java and Southeast Asian prototypes.

A number of excavations have been carried out at Lalitagiri, by the Archeological Survey of India. Among them, the most prominent one is that of an ancient stupa. The stupa is said to contain relics preserved in caskets of stone. Because of the age of the relics, as well as their silver and gold contents, it is alleged that they belong to Lord Buddha. Other excavations include black polished inscribed pieces of pottery of Ashokan Brahmi script, Kushan inscriptions, ornamental Brahmi, etc.

All these artifacts have further strengthened the notion that Lalitagiri was once a flourishing Buddhist center. A number of monuments have also been unearthed at Lalitagiri. Of them, the most significant ones consist of the ruins of an apsidal temple, encircled by monasteries and stupas. The recent excavations at Lalitagiri have been linked to the Gandharva School of art.

Ratnagiri

The city of Ratnagiri is situated in the in Jajpur district of Orissa, India. It lies at a distance of approximately 100 km from Bhubaneshwar city. The city stands encircled by rivers, namely Mahanadi, Brahmani, Kimiria and Birupa, in all the directions. A number of excavations have been carried out at Ratnagiri and they have dated the city to the period of the Gupta dynasty, i.e., somewhere around the 6th century AD. Numerous Buddhist structures were unearthed form the hill range nearby.

One of the excavations came out with a massive monastery, believed to be of the Mahayana sect. Apart from the monastery, numerous other items were unearthed, including stupas, chaityas, etc. Ratnagiri also holds the distinction of being a great learning center of the Buddhism of Tantric cult, known as Vajrayana. It has also been mentioned in the Tibetan Buddhist texts that the city witnessed the prosperity of the Kalchakrayana.

Udaigiri

These caves were found to contain some of the most antique and architecturally significant Buddhist sculptures. Some of them are

Bodhisattva figures, while others have Buddha in a meditating position. Ancient Buddhist monasteries, stupas and other items found here symbolize the rich history of the city. Even the hills forming the backdrop of the excavations stand adorned with inscriptions and rock cut sculptures.

Kapilvastu

Kapilvastu is located at a distance of 27 kilometers south of Lumbini Gardens close to district of Siddhartha Nagar in Uttar Pradesh. The place is positioned close to both Lumbini as well as Shravasti. Kapilvastu was the capital of the Shakya household where Lord Buddha or Gautama Buddha was born to King Shuddhodhana. He grew up amidst lavishness and was kept away from the miseries of life. But suddenly one day he broke away the comfortable trap of his father and set out for a journey on his own. The place is important to envision as the pre contemplation, luxurious days of the Lord who had bestowed much upon humanity by giving up his own luxury and princely class.

The Tourist Attractions in Kapilvastu are innumerable and the beauty and charm of Kapilvastu are sure to captivate all kinds of tourists.

Kapilvastu is a primary archeological location and for this reason it is one of the most frequently visited tourist destinations in Nepal. The place has the ruins of the citadel where Lord Buddha spent his formative years. The archeological works that had been done in this area had to go through various barriers including monetary limitation. The archaeologists had excavated out as many as 14 different layers of human habitat in this region. The oldest among the human habitations dates back to 8th Century BC. There are many Stupas spread across the place, built by Ashoka and the Gupta Kings. The symbols left behind by the Shakya dynasty are clearly seen and there are relics of Lord Buddha himself. Excavations carried out by the Archaeological survey of India relate Kapil Vastu to the Kushan period. The excavations include a stupa, of an ancient monastery named Devaputra, and two mounds, regarded as the ruins of King Suddhodhana's palace. Other major attractions of Kapilvastu include stupas built by Ashoka and the Gupta Kings, relics of Lord Buddha, etc.

Kaushambi

The district of Kaushambi is situated in Uttar Pradesh. It was the erstwhile capital of 'Vatsa Janpad', during the time of Buddha and came under the reign of King Udyana. Kaushambi also holds the distinction of serving as the host to Lord Buddha, in the 6th and 9th year after his enlig. It also had the good luck of being the place where Buddha delivered a number of sermons, thus elevating it to the status of a learning center for Buddhists.

A number of archaeological excavations have been carried out in Kaushambi. These excavations have led to the discovery of numerous sculptures, figurines, coins, punch-marked, cast coins, terra-cotta sculptures, etc. Other major attractions of Kaushambi include an Ashokan Pillar, an old fort and the Ghositaram Monastery. The monastery is believed to have been built by a wealthy merchant of the city. A large number of architectural relics and ruins also came up during the excavations. There are also a number of stupas in Kaushambi, India. Of them, the most impressive one is 25 m in diameter and 25 m in length. It dates back to the 5th century BC.

Mathura

The city of Mathura is situated on the western bank of the river Yamuna, in Uttar Pradesh. It lies at a distance of approximately 145 km from Delhi, the capital of India, and 58 km from Agra, the city of Taj. The city holds the distinction of being the birthplace of Lord Krishna, a Hindu God. Along with being a major Hindu pilgrimage, Mathura is also one of the prominent Buddhist sites in India. It also had the fortuity of hosting Lord Buddha, once in His lifetime. Even after His mahaparinirvana, Mathura prospered as a major Buddhist center, till about 9th century CE. Mahakachhayana, a distinguished scholar and a disciple of the Buddha, was responsible for sermonizing the thoughts and principles of Buddhism to the people of Mathura. With the construction of a monastic complex in Mathura by Upagupta, the religious teacher of Emperor Ashoka, the religion started budding in the city. During that time, Mathura school of art also flourished here, which became a famous attribute of the Buddha's sculptures.

There have been references of about twenty Buddhist monasteries, three stupas and five Deva temples in Mathura. However, by the 11th century, Buddhism started declining in the city.

Prabhosa

Prabhosa is situated in the state of Uttar Pradesh. It lies at a distance of approximately one kilometer from the district of Kaushambi in India. In the ancient times, this place was known as Mankula. The significance of Prabhosa is that it served as the venue of the 6th rain retreat of Lord Buddha. However, it could not have the fortuity of receiving religious sermons by Buddha. Prabhosa boasts of a number of caves and rock shelters. The largest cave is known as Sita's Window. It is believed that Buddha stayed in this cave only, when he visited Prabhosa.

Hieun Tsang, the famous Chinese traveler, also visited this place in the 7th century AD. In the account of his travels in India, Hieun Tsang has even made a reference about a stupa being constructed there, by Emperor Ashoka. However, presently no Buddhist antiquities are housed here.

Sravasti

Sravasti is situated in the Gonda district of Uttar Pradesh. It was the erstwhile capital of the ancient kingdom of Kosala Mahajanapada. It is believed that Sravasti, also known as Sahet-Mahet, was founded by the legendary king Sravast. This place is important from Buddhism point of view because Lord Buddha performed a number of miracles here. It was in Sravasti that He displayed a million fold manifestation of himself. He was seated on a lotus (with thousand petals), with fire and water radiating from His body.

The magical feats exhibited by Lord, while sitting on the lotus, are still narrated by the people of Sravasti. The town also had the fortuity of playing host to Lord Buddha for 24 rainy seasons in the Jetvana Gardens. All the stories associated with Sravasti seem to establish Lord Buddha as a divine personality. Even though there is no evidence for most of the stories related to Sravasti, still the place attracts tourists from far and wide. Age-old stupas, splendid monasteries and a number of temples add to the appeal of Sravasti.

Bharhut Stupa

(The Śunga-Andhra epoch (2nd-1st Century B.C.) was one of the most creative periods of Buddhist art. Though the Sunga rulers were followers of the Brahmanical faith and Buddhism was deprived of the State patronage which it enjoyed during the reign of the Mauryan rulers, like Asoka and some of his successors, there was no set-back in the propagation or popularity of the Buddhist faith. (Buddhist establishments flourished in Bodh-Gaya, Bharhut, and Sanchi in Northern and Central India, in Amaravati and Jaggayapeta in South India, at Bhaja, Nasik, Karle and Janta and at several other places in Western India. The art of this period consists mainly in the excavation of the rock-cut temples or viharas (some of which are embellished with paintings) and the erection of railings and toranas (gateways) to the Buddhist Stupas at different places). General Cunningham found remains of the railings and on gateway of the Stupa at Bharhut (Madhya Pradesh) during the years 1872-74 and had them deposited in the Indian Museum in the year following. The Stupa in question was built during the 2nd Century B.C. In the absence of the Stupa itself it is difficult to ascertain its shape and size. But it was probably similar to the Stupas represented on its panels and the almost contemporary Stupas of Sanchi. All these Stupas consist of hemispherical dome with a harmika above suppporting the umbrellas.

One of the main interest of the Bharhut sculptures consists in the representation of the birth-stories of the Gautama Budha. These stories (or the Jatakas) are of two main classes, those relating to the previous births of Buddha as a Bodhisattva (a Buddha potentia), and those of his last appearance as Gautama Shakyamuni when he attained Enlightenment of Buddhahood. The Jatakas represented on the Bharhut panels include Mahakapi-Jataka, Latuva-Jataka, Miga-Jataka, Sujata-gahuto-Jataka, Mahajanaka-Jataka and Vidhurapandita-Jataka, Chhadanta Jataka, etc.

The scenes on the Bharhut sculptures, relating to the life of Gautama Shakyamuni include, among others, the dream of Maya (Illustrating the descent of a Bodhisattva in the form of an elephant into the mothers womb), the defeat of Mara, Gautama's Enlightenment under the Bodhi tree, the worship of the Bodhi tree, the worship of Gautama's hair-locks by celestial beings, the visits of king Ajatashatru of Magadha and of Prasenjit of Koshala, etc.

The worship of the Bodhi tree, seems to have been widely prevalent, as there are many representation of it on the sculptured panels of Bharhut, Sanchi and Amaravati. Again, in the Divyavandana it is related that the Bodhi tree was Asoka's favourite object of worship. The lowest architrave of the Eastern Gateway Stupa I, Sanchi (1st Century B.C.) depicts the ceremonial visits of king Asoka and his queen, Tishyarakshita to the Bodhi Tree. In the centre of the panel are the tree and the temple of Bodh Gaya. On the left is seen a crowd of musicians and devotees carrying water vessels. On the right are the king and the queen descending from the elephant and payment homage to the Bodhi tree.

Sanchi

The Stupas at Sanchi

Sanchi is situated in the state of Madhya Pradesh in India. It lies at a distance of approximately 52 km from the capital city of Bhopal and 10 km from Vidisha. The major attractions of Sanchi include a number of Buddhiststupas, monasteries, temples and pillars. All these structures date back to somewhere between 3rd century BC and 12th century AD. The Mauryan emperor Ashoka founded all the stupas at Sanchi in the honor of Lord Buddha.

They have the distinction of being included by UNESCO in its list of World Heritage Sites.

However, the most magnificent as well as the largest one of these is the "Great Stupa of Sanchi". One of the best-preserved stupas, it is also the oldest of the existing structures in India, dating back to the Buddhist period. Encircling the Great Sanchi Stupa is a railing, with four carved gateways, each facing one of the four directions. It is believed that these gateways were carved around 100 AD. All the stupas at Sanchi, Madhya Pradesh, have a unique feature of not having any images of Lord Buddha in human form.

Instead, Buddha has been illustrated symbolically, in the form of inanimate figures. The figures include wheels (representing his teaching), his footprints, empty throne etc. However, the figure that is most extensively used consists of a lotus flower. In Buddhism, lotus has a special meaning attached to it. It is both a beautiful decoration as well as a religious symbol. Buddhists believe that, like lotus grows from mud to produce a beautiful white blossom, people can also emerge from the mud of materialism into sunlight.

The exquisite carvings on these stupas depict a world where humans and animals live in perfect harmony with each other. The gateways of all the stupas have carvings that portray a number of incidents from the life of the Buddha as well as his previous incarnations as Bodhisattvas described in Jataka tales. Then, you have the male and female tree spirits adorned on the stupa gateways. The female tree spirits symbolize fertility and are used by Buddhists as welcoming figures.

Dharamsala

The town of Dharamsala is situated in Himachal Pradesh, on the high slopes in the upper reaches of Kangra Valley. With the

Dhauladhar Mountains serving as its backdrop, the town presents a picturesque sight. Dharamsala is divided into two parts, the Upper Dharamsala and the Lower Dharamsala, differing by approximately 1000 m in altitude. The town serves as the headquarters of the Tibetan government in exile. Dharamshala is also the seat of His Holiness, The 14th Dalai Lama in India.

Prayer Wheels at Buddhist Temple in the Dalai Lama's Home Town of Dharamsala

It houses a large settlement of Tibetan refugee. Monks in their robes and old Tibetans walking with rosaries in their hands or turning the prayer wheels is a common sight here. There are a number of monasteries and temples in Dharamsala, which serves as the major attractions for the tourists coming here. There are also several institutes here, set up to conserve the art, culture and traditions of Tibet.

McLeodganj

The town of McLeodganj is situated in Himachal Pradesh, India. The town dates back to the mid 19th century when it was established as a British garrison. Mcleodganj was initially the home of the semi-nomadic Gaddi tribe. Today, it serves as the residence of His Holiness, The 14th Dalai Lama - Tenzin Gyatso. However, even now, a considerable number of Gaddi families live in the villages around Mcleod Ganj.

Residence of the Dalai Lama

The Dalai Lama lives on the south edge of town. He came to Macleod Ganj in the year 1960 and since then, he has been living here only. Most of his house has been transformed into government offices, while he occupies only a small portion of the entire complex.

Tsuglagkhang

Tsuglagkhang, the main Buddhist temple of Dharamsala, is situated just opposite the private residence of The Dalai Lama. It houses the images of Shakyamuni, Padmasambhava and Avalokitesvara, all of them sitting in meditation postures.

Gompa Dip Tse-Chok Ling

Gompa Dip Tse-Chok Ling is a small monastery situated at the foot of a sharp road. The main prayer hall of the monastery is adorned with the image of Shakyamuni. The other attractions of the monastery include its beautiful and intricate mandals.

Library of Tibetan Works and Archives

There is also a library of Tibetan works and archives in McLeodganj. It comprises of a rich collection of almost 40 per cent of the original Tibetan manuscripts. There is also a photographic archive in the library.

Pilak

Pilak is situated in the state of Tripura, surrounded by flourishing green valley speckled with paddy fields. It lies at a distance of approximately 100 km from the capital city of Agartala. The city is sparsely populated and serves as the gateway to the rich bygone era of the state. Pilak is significant as a pilgrim destination in India, from both Hinduism as well as Buddhism point of view. One of the major attractions of the city are the archaeological remains found here, which date back to somewhere around eighth and ninth century AD.

One can find some of the most exquisite Hindu and Buddhist sculptures at Pilak in Tripura. The relics unearthed at Pilak include terracotta plaques, sealing with Stupa, huge stone images of Avolokiteswara and Narasimha, etc. The plaques and the sealing signify survival of heterodox creeds and sects representing both Hinduism as well as Buddhism.

9
Mahaparinirvan Express

Most travellers in India and abroad must have heard of Palace on Wheel. It is rated as one of the 'ten best rail journeys in the world'. This luxury train takes us on a seven-day visit to medieval forts and palaces of Rajasthan. Going by its success, while Gujarat launched 'Royal Orient Express' Maharashtra launched 'Deccan Queen'. Since most places associated Lord Buddha's life are located in the interior part of north-central India, Ministry of Tourism mulled over an idea of connecting them with a similar train service and did a pilot run of a 'Buddhist Special' train in 1999. But it was discontinued after the first run.

Further, in an attempt to give a new meaning to pilgrim tourism in India, Indian Railway Catering and Tourism Corporation (IRCTC) has launched a special train named Mahaparinirvan Express in 2007, for Buddhist pilgrims from India and abroad particularly from the South Asian countries. This will provide the first major link to all Buddhist pilgrim spots in India and Nepal in the environs of luxury and comfort. The train will take passengers to important destinations linked to the life of Buddha such as Bodh Gaya, Rajgir, Nalanda, Kushinagar, Lumbini, Sravasti. The package includes train travel, road travel, all meals, deluxe hotel facilities, sightseeing, monument entry fees, security, insurance and guide services. But the beauty of the entire package is that once passengers boarded the train everything was taken care of by the Railways. As the journey includes a day trip to Nepal, those who aren't Indian nationals will need a Nepali visa. This can easily be obtained at the border. Two passport sized photographs are required. Foreign tourists with Indian visas must make sure that these are double or multiple entry visas, so that return to India will be allowed. The special train will have 3 coches of first AC, 3 coaches of two-tier AC and 1 coach of three-tier AC. The fare from October 2008 to March 2009 will be US$ 150, 125 and 95 for 1st AC, 2nd AC and 3rd AC respectively per person per night on twin sharing basis. The travel related information for this train has been prepared in Japanese, Korean, Chinese and Thai languages for the convenience of international travellers. Indian passengers can pay in equivalent Rupee (INR) amount, at the exchange rate prevalent at the time of payment.

Salient Features of Mahaparinirvan Special Tour

1. *Exclusive Train for Mahaparinirvan Tour*

The Maha Parinirvan Special Tour Train is an exclusive air conditioned train and does not carry passengers other than those booked with IRCTC for this special tour.

2. *Security on Train*

Private Security Guards in each coach.

3. *On-board Hygienic Kitchen Car Facility*

The passengers can choose from an assortment of sumptuous hot meals (Veg / Non Veg), snacks and cold drinks. Packaged drinking water, tea and coffee are also available to the passengers in ample quantity.

4. *On-board Clean and Hygienic Lavatories and Showers*

For the convenience of the passengers, clean and hygienic lavatories and showers are provided on-board.

5. *Accommodation in Comfortable Hotels of the Buddhist Circuit*

Accommodation in comfortable hotels of the Buddhist Circuit.

6. *Visa Facilitation for Lumbini*

For visiting Lumbini (Nepal), acquiring the Nepal visa is facilitated by IRCTC. The passenger needs to carry the requisite documents, photographs etc. It is, however, recommended that tourists should obtain the visa in advance before arriving in India.

7. *Insurance Cover*

All passengers are provided with Comprehensive Insurance Cover for the duration of the tour.

8. *Medical Facility*

In case of any exigency, medical support can be provided through an extensive network of Indian Railways medical facilities.

9. *Language Guide*

On sufficient advance information, tour guides of various languages would be provided for sizeable groups.

Places Covered by Mahaparinirvan Express

Gaya

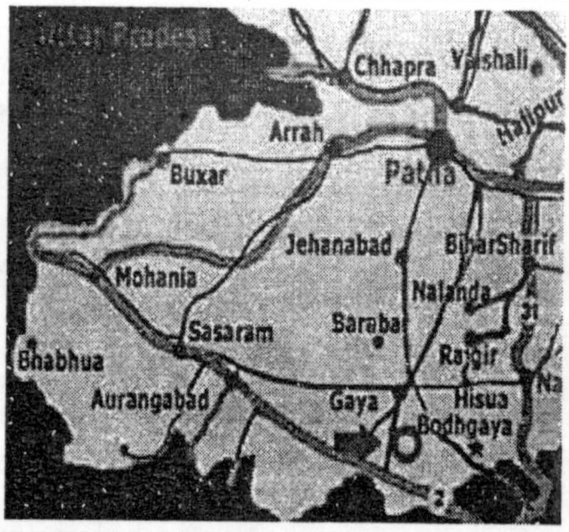

Gaya derives its name from the mythological demon Gayasur (which literally means Gaya the holy demon), demon (asur, a Sanskrit word) and Gaya. Lord Vishnu killed Gayasur, the holy demon by using the pressure of his foot over him. This incident transformed Gayasur into the series of rocky hills that make up the landscape of the Gaya city. Gaya was so holy that he had the power to absolve the sins of those who touched him or looked at him; after his death many people have flocked to Gaya to perform shraddha sacrifices on his body to absolve the sins of their ancestors. The most popular temple today is Vishnupad Temple, a place along the Falgu River, marked by a footprint of Vishnu incised into a block of basalt that marks the act of Lord Vishnu subduing Gayasur by placing his foot on Gayasurs chest. Buddhist tradition regards the footstep in the Vishnupad Temple as a footstep of Buddha. For Buddhists, Gaya is an important pilgrimage place because it was at Brahmayoni hill that Buddha preached the Fire Sermon (Adittapariyaya Sutta) to one thousand former fire-worshipping ascetics, who all became enlightened while listening to this discourse. At that time, the hill was called Gayasisa.

Bodhgaya

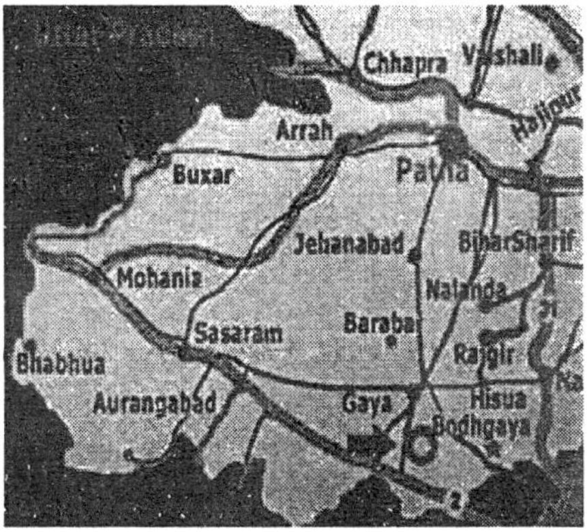

According to Buddhist traditions, 500 BC Prince Gautama Siddhartha, wandering as a monk, reached the sylvan banks of Falgu River, near the city of Gaya. There he sat in meditation under a bodhi tree. After three days and three nights of meditation, Siddhartha attained enlightenment and insight, and the answers that he had sought. He then spent seven weeks at seven different spots in the vicinity meditating and considering his experience. After seven weeks, he traveled to Sarnath, where he began teaching Buddhism.

Disciples of Gautama Siddhartha began to visit the place where he had gained enlightenment during the full moon in the month of Vaisakh (April-May), as per the Hindu calendar. Over time, the place became known as Bodhgaya, the day of enlightenment as Buddha Purnima, and the tree as the Bodhi Tree.

As the place of the Buddhas Enlightenment, Bodhgaya is the spiritual home of Buddhists. Located in Bihar, 115 kms from Patna, the land is rich and fertile, dotted with green fields and watered by the river Phalgu - the same ancient Nairanjana River where the Buddha bathed after attaining enlightenment. A range of low forested hills silhouette the small hamlets flanking the glistening, sandy banks of the river. Monks and nuns rub shoulders with tourists and believers from all over the world. An all-pervading calm envelops the town, giving visitors a sense of peace.

Rajgir

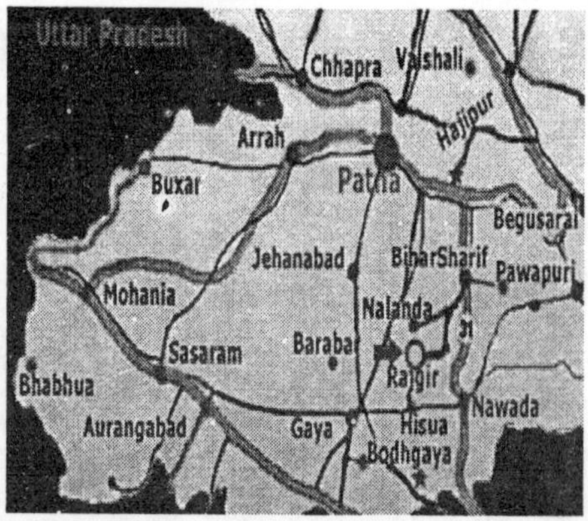

The meandering river Banganga and five hills ensconce picturesque Rajgir, ancient Rajgriha (literally, the abode of kings). During the lifetime of the Buddha this was the capital of the powerful Magadhan kingdom, ruled by the virtuous king Bimbisara. Like many others in search of Truth, Prince Siddhartha, after he renounced his royal heritage came to this city to seek the path of salvation. Later, he overwhelmed the citizens of Rajagriha with his serenity and grace and converted King Bimbisara of Magadha and countless others to his religion. The hills and caves surrounding

Rajagriha were home to spiritual teachers, ranging from the materialism of the early Charavaka School to the metaphysics of Upanishadic philosophers. In fact the first Buddhist council after the Buddha was hosted here at the Saptaparni caves. It was Rajgir which saw Gautam Buddha spending several months meditating, and preaching at Griddhkuta, ('Hill of the Vultures'). He also delivered some of his famous sermons. The rich merchant community here soon became the Buddhas followers and built many structures of typical Buddhist architecture.

Nalanda

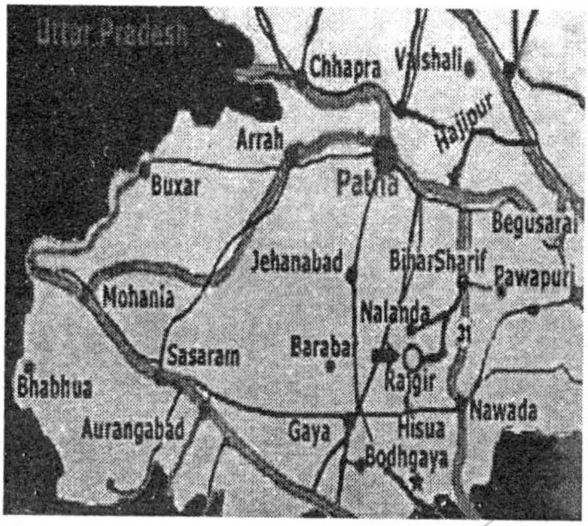

Naland—the most renowned university in ancient India derived its name from Na-alam-da, meaning Insatiable in Giving, one of the names by which the Lord Buddha was known. Nalanda was one of the world's first residential universities, i.e., it had dormitories for students. In its heyday it accommodated over 10,000 students and 2,000 teachers. The university was considered an architectural masterpiece, and was marked by a lofty wall and one gate. The subjects taught at Nalanda University covered every field of learning, and it attracted pupils and scholars from Korea, Japan, China, Tibet, Indonesia, Persia and Turkey.

The Buddha is mentioned as having several times stayed at Nalanda. When he visited Nalanda he would usually reside in Pavarikas mango grove, and while there he had discussions with Upali-Gahapati and Dighatapassi, with Kevatta, and also several conversations with Asibandhakaputta. The Buddha visited Nalanda during his last tour through Magadha, and it was there that Sariputta uttered his lions roar, affirming his faith in the Buddha, shortly before his death. Also, Nalanda was the residence of Sonnadinna. Mahavira is several times mentioned as staying at Nalanda, which was evidently a centre of activity of the Jains.

Varanasi

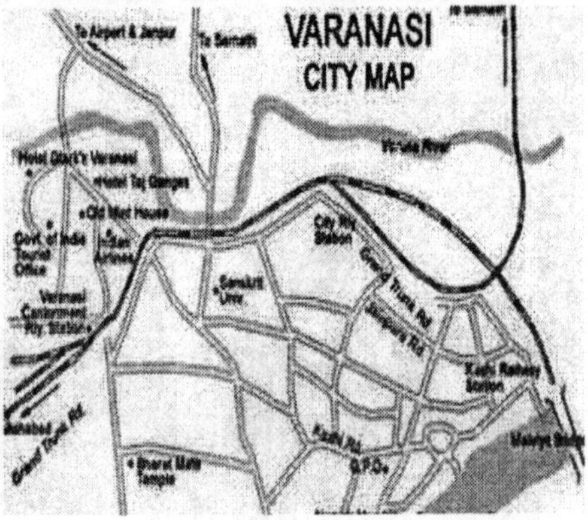

The city of Varanasi is situated along the west bank of the Ganges in the north Indian state of Uttar Pradesh. Called Benaras by the British, Varanasi is a holy city in Hinduism, being one of the most sacred pilgrimage places for Hindus of all denominations. More than 1,000,000 pilgrims visit the city each year. The city finds mention in the great epics of Mahabharata and Ramayana. The renowned American novelist Mark Twain once wrote, "Benaras is older than history, older than tradition, older even than legend and looks twice as old as all of them put together." It has the holy shrine of Lord Kashi Vishwanath (a manifestation of Lord Shiva), and also one of the twelve revered Jyotirlingas of Lord Shiva. According to mythology, Lord Shiva once in fact lived in Kashi (Varanasi). Hindus believe that bathing in Ganga remits sins and that dying in Kashi ensures release of a person's soul from the cycle of its transmigrations.

Varanasi is one of the holiest places in Buddhism too. It was believed that over twenty-five centuries ago, a sage travelled 200 kms from Bodhgaya, where he had attained Nirvana to reach the ghats of Varanasi of Kashi as it was then called. The city had seen saffron clad spiritual teachers before him, who came here, drawn by its magnetic, inexplicable spiritual power. The Sage was looking for five Hindu ascetics, old companions from whom he had parted, because they had insisted that the only path to salvation was through self-mortification. The Buddha found them at Rishipattana, the Deer park near Kashi, and gave them the gift of the spiritual knowledge which he had attained since he parted with them, and they became his first followers, and the first members of the Sangha.

Sarnath

Sarnath is located 13 kilometres north-east of Varanasi, in Uttar Pradesh, India. It Sarnath (also Mrigadava, Migadaya, Rishipattana, Isipatana) is the deer park where Gautama Buddha first taught the Dharma, and where the Buddhist Sangha came into existence through the enlightenment of Kondanna. Gautama Buddha started teaching not to debate but for the advantage of and out of compassion for human beings. He explained the middle way which avoids extremes, the Four Noble Truths, and prescribed the Eight-fold path.

There are remains dating as far back as the 3rd century B.C. when Emperor Ashoka founded various institutions, stupas, monasteries and pillar edicts. The runs at Sarnath and the art collection in the Archaeological Museum are representations/ examples of the glorious past of Sarnath. Archaeological remains are open from Sunrise to Sunset.

Gorakhpur

Gorakhpur is a city in the eastern part of the state of Uttar Pradesh in India, near the border with Nepal. It is the administrative headquarters of Gorakhpur District and Gorakhpur Division. Gorakhpur is famous as a religious centre: the city was home to Buddhist, Hindu, Jain and Sikh saints and is named after the medieval saint Gorakshanath. The city is also home to many historic Buddhist sites.

Gautama Buddha, founder of Buddhism, renounced his princely clothing at the confluence of the rivers Rapti and Rohini, near Gorakhpur, before setting out on his quest of truth in 600 BC. The city is also associated with the travels of Lord Buddhas contemporary Lord Mahavira, the 24th Tirthankara of Jainism.

Kushinagar

At this location, near the Hiranyavati River, Gautama Buddha attained Parinirvana (or Final Nirvana) after falling ill from eating a meal of a species of mushroom. It is said that the Buddha had three reasons for coming to Kusinárá to die.

1. Because it was the proper venue for the preaching of the Mahá-Sudassana Sutta;

2. Because Subhadda would visit him there and, after listening to his sermon, would develop meditation and become an arahant while the Buddha was still alive; and

3. Because the brahman Doha would be there, after the Buddhas death, to solve the problem of the distribution of his relics. As the scene of his death, Kusinara became one of the four holy places declared by the Buddha (in the Mahaparinibbana Sutta) to be fit places of pilgrimage for the pious, the other three being Kapilavatthu, Buddhagaya and Isipatana.

Lumbini (Nepal)

Lumbini (meaning "the lovely") is a Buddhist pilgrimage site located in Rupandehi District, Lumbini Zone of Nepal, near the Indian border. It is the place where Mayadevi gave birth to Siddhartha Gautama, who later became a Buddha (Gautama Buddha), and founded the religion of Buddhism. Gautama Buddha lived between approximately 563 BCE and 483 BCE. For Buddhists, this is one of the four main pilgrimage sites based around the life of Gautama Buddha, the other three being Kushinagar, Bodhgaya, and Sarnath.

Lumbini is located 25 km east of the municipality of Kapilavastu, the place where the Buddha grew up and lived up to the age of 29. Kapilvastu is the name of place as well as the neighbouring district. Lumbini has various Buddhist temples including the Mayadevi temple. There is also the Puskarini pond and remains of Kapilvastu palace in Lumbini. There are other sites near Lumbini where, according to Buddhist tradition, previous Buddhas were born and achieved enlightenment and died.

Sravasti

Sravasti, the capital of the ancient kingdom of Kosala, has the honour for sheltering Buddha for 24 rainy seasons in the Jetvana Gardens. The city believed to be founded by the mythological king Sravast, has age-old stupas, majestic monasteries and several temples. Buddha is said to have performed some miracles here.

This holy place also has the famous Anand Bodhi tree, an offspring of the one, said to have been planted by Buddhas main disciple. Another famous incident in Sravasti was - during the time of Sakyamuni, Sudatta, a rich and pious merchant, lived in Sravasti. While on a visit to Rajgir, he heard the Buddha's sermon and decided to become the Lords disciple. But he was caught in dilemma and asked the Lord whether he could become a follower without forsaking worldly life. To his query, the Master replied that it was enough that he followed his vocation in a righteous manner.

Agra

Agra's Taj Mahal is one of the most famous buildings in the world, the mausoleum of Shah Jahan's favourite wife, Mumtaz Mahal. It is one of the New 7 Wonders of the world, and one of three World Heritage Sites in Agra, the others being Agra Fort and Fatehpur Sikri.

Completed in 1653 A.D., the Taj Mahal is believed to be built by the Mughal Badshah (king) Shah Jahan as the final resting place for his beloved wife, Mumtaz. Finished in marble, it is perhaps Indias most fascinating and beautiful monument. This perfectly symmetrical monument took 22 years (1630-1652) of hard labour and 20,000 workers, masons and jewellers to build and is set amidst landscaped gardens. Built by the Persian architect, Ustad Isa, the Taj Mahal is on the bank of the Yamuna River. It can be observed like a mirage from the Agra Fort from where Emperor Shah Jahan stared at it, for the last eight years his life as a prisoner of his son Aurangzeb. It is a masterpiece of symmetry, seeming to be floating in the air from a distance, and each revealed as an illusion experienced as one enters through the main gate. Verses of the Holy Koran are inscribed on it and at the top of gate 22 small domes, signifying the number of years the monument took to build. The Taj Mahal was built on a marble platform that stands above a sandstone one. The most elegant dome of the Taj, with a diameter of 60 feet, rises 80 feet over the building and directly under the dome is the tomb of Mumtaz Mahal. Shah Jahans tomb was erected next to hers by his son Aurangzeb. Fantastic inlay works using semi-precious stones decorate the interiors.

Itinerary of Mahaparinirvan Express

Day	*Sector*	*Programme*
		DAY–I
Day 1	Delhi–Gaya (990 kms)	14:30 hrs.–Assemble at the Delhi Safdurjung Railway Station. Traditional Welcome and check–in to your respective coaches. 16:00 hrs.–Departure of the train for Gaya. Evening Tea & Dinner served on-board. Overnight stay on-board.
		DAY–II
Day 2	Gaya – Bodhgaya (16 kms)	Arrive at Gaya Railway Station early morning. Disembark and assemble for boarding the coaches for road journey of approx one hour to Bodhgaya. Arrive at Bodhgaya Hotel and check-in. Wash &
		Contd...

Day	*Sector*	*Programme*
		Change, followed by the breakfast. After breakfast proceed by coach for sightseeing of Bodhgaya including Mahabodhi Temple and Niranjana River. Return to the Hotel for lunch and relax for some time. Proceed for sightseeing of Thai Temple, Japanese Temple and Buddha Statue. Evening. – Return to Hotel, dinner and overnight stay at hotel in Bodhgaya. **DAY–III**
Day 3	Bodhgaya–Nalanda–Rajgir–Gaya–Varanasi	05:00 hrs.–Early morning tea and breakfast followed by checkout from the Hotel. Departure for Rajgir by bus (85 kms). 10:30 hrs.–Arrival at Rajgir. Sightseeing at Rajgir of Bimbimsara Jail, Gridhakut hill, Venuvan. 12:30 hrs.–Proceed to a Restaurant in Rajgir for lunch. After lunch, proceed to Nalanda for sightseeing covering ruins of world famous Nalanda University and Nalanda Museum. 16:00 hrs.–Depart back to Gaya Railway Station.
		Contd...

Day	*Sector*	*Programme*
		20:00 hrs.–Arrival at Gaya Railway Station and board the train. Dinner on-board. Departure from Gaya at 2330 hrs to Varanasi (220 kms) by train. Overnight stay on-board.
		DAY–IV
Day 4	Varanasi–Sarnath–Gorakhpur	Early morning tea on-board and arrival at Varanasi. Proceed to the hotel for wash and change and breakfast. After breakfast, visit Sarnath (10 kms) for to see Dhamekh Stupa, Sarnath Museum, The Ashokan Pillar, Mulgandha Kuti Vihar. Afternoon–Lunch at the hotel. Followed by some free time. Tourists can either opt for shopping or other activities. Evening–Visit to the river Ganges Ghat, Boat ride, Evening Arti. Return to the Train. 20:00 hrs.–Arrival at the Varanasi Railway Station and board the train Dinner on board. Departure for Gorakhpur (224 kms) at 23:30 hrs. Overnight stay on-board.

Contd...

Day	*Sector*	*Programme*
		DAY–V
Day 5	Gorakhpur–Kushinagar	Early morning tea on board. Arrive at Gorakhpur Railway Station. Proceed by coach to Hotel at Kushinagar. Arrive at the Hotel in Kushinagar and check-in. Breakfast at the Hotel. After breakfast, visit Mahaparinirvan Temple, Rambhar Stupa, Mata Kutir Temple etc. Afternoon – Lunch at the Hotel. Evening participate in a chanting and meditation session. (Subject to availability of appropriate teachers). Dinner and overnight stay at Hotel.
		DAY–VI
Day 6	Kushinagar–Lumbini–Gorakhpur	05:00 hrs. : Early morning tea and breakfast at the hotel. 06:00 hrs.–Check-out of the Hotel and proceed to Lumbini. (Nepal) by bus. Tourists must obtain the Nepal visa from their respective countries. Otherwise, lot of time required at the border to process the visa. Arrive Lumbini and proceed to a hotel/restaurant for Lunch.
		Contd...

Day	*Sector*	*Programme*
		Visit Lumbini including Maya Devi Temple, Ashokan Pillar and Pushkarni lake. 16:00 hrs–Departure for Gorakhpur. Arrive Gorakhpur Railway Station. Board at around 20:30 hrs and board the Train. Dinner on-board, Depart by train to Gonda at 23:30 hrs. Overnight stay on-board.
		DAY–VII
Day 7	Gonda–Sravasti–Gonda–Agra	Early morning tea on-board and arrival at Gonda Railway Station. Departure for Sravasti (65 kms) by bus. Arrival at the hotel, wash & change and breakfast. After breakfast, visit Jetvana Vihara, Pakki Kuti & Sehat Mahet, Thai Temple. Afternoon–Lunch at the Hotel and proceed to back to Gonda railway station to board the train. 16:30 hrs–Arrival at the Gonda Railway Station to board the Train. Depart by train to Agra (450 kms) at 18:00 hrs. Evening Tea and dinner served on-board. Overnight stay on-board.
		Contd...

Day	*Sector*	*Programme*
		DAY–VIII
Day 8	Agra – Delhi	Early morning on-board tea and arrival at Agra. Proceed to hotel for Wash and Fresh and Breakfast. After breakfast, proceed for the sight-seeing of the World famous Taj Mahal. 12:30 hrs.–Proceed to the Agra Railway Station. Departure by train for New Delhi (220 kms) at 14:15 hrs. Onboard lunch and evening tea. Arrival at the Delhi Safdurjung Railway Station. Around 18:00 hrs.

For information and booking, one can contact the following:

Email: tourticket@irctc.co.in or Market Office of IRCTC, 2nd Floor, STC Building, Jawahar Vyapar Bhawan, 1-Tolstoy Marg, New Delhi-110001. Tel./Fax: 011-23701174, 23701145-47.

10
Conclusion

Even after 2500 years of his Mahaparinirvan, the teachings of Lord Buddha continue to inspire the generations to liberate themselves from worldly suffering. What is more interesting is that Buddha never proclaimed that he has found a new religion. He said "to practice my teaching one need not always take to renunciation. One can diligently practice the same with the worldly chores and reap the same benefits, because it is a way of life". Contribution of Buddhism has come in more than one way. The cave paintings of Ajanta are still admired by Generation Y and the rock edicts formed the foundation of a welfare state. In fact, Indian constitution draws so heavily from the Buddhism principles that without a study of the Buddhist philosophy one can hardly comprehend the precepts of our constitution.

However, in our country of one billion plus citizens, only 8 million practice Buddhism as a religion. Sadly, the religion which crossed boundaries and became the principal religion of most developed south-east Asian nations has lost its ground in India, its birthplace. And perhaps this could be one of the reasons of India's economic backwardness. But we have a wonderful opportunity now. For these 1.6 billion people in world who follow Buddhism as a religion, coming to visit places associated with Lord Buddha is the most sacred of the pilgrimages. We must cash on opportunity and make the places associated with Buddhism more accessible and provide adequate amenities so that a visitor would either repeat his visits to India to know more or refer it to others. The

Ministry of Tourism (MoT) in its 'Look East Policy' had already endorsed this fact and is open to ideas that consolidate it further. One such initiative is *Mahaparinirvan Express* by IRCTC, under Ministry of Railways.

Those who are pressed for time can take the readymade package offered by *Mahaparinirvan Express*, without having to worry about the minute details of tour planning. The package takes care of one's travel, accommodation, catering, sightseeing and in fact, everything – of course, for a price. On the other hand if one wants to have a firsthand experience of the 'path to liberation', one can join a 12-day residential meditation course with the Vipassana Sadhana Sansthan. Learn the technique and practice for rest of the life. This course is taught free and the establishment expenditures are met with the donations from the previous participants who out of their compassion would like others to learn this 'path of liberation'.

Thanks to *Samrat Asoka* and other yesteryear emperors who patronised Buddhism, there is either a cave or a rock edict or monastery in the close vicinity of each town or village in our country. Thus, each one of us must take some time out of our busy schedule to walk in the footsteps of Lord Buddha i.e. visit the places associated with Buddhism and Lord Buddha. Last but not the least, in today's world of violence and intolerance, Lord Buddha's teaching have become more relevant. Let us strive to make this world a better place to live for our future generations.

BHAVATU SABBA MANGALAM !!!

(May all beings be happy !!!)

Bibliography

Zen Buddhism: Daisetz T. Suzuki.

The Buddha on meditation and states of consciouseness: Danie J. Goleman.

Essence of Buddhism: Traleg Kyabgon.

Simple Buddhism: A Guide to Enlightened Living: Drs. C. Alexander and Annellen Simpkins.

Buddhism for Busy People: Finding Happiness in an Uncertain World: David Michie.

Buddha: A Story of Enlightenment: Deepak Chopra.

The Ajanta Caves: Ancient Paintings of Buddhist India: Benoy K. Behl.

The Cave Temples of India: Fergusson, James & Burgess, James.

History of Theravada Buddhism in South-East Asia with Special Reference to India and Ceylon: Hazra, Kanai Lal.

Vipassana The Buddhist Way: by Sobti.

A Guide to Boddhisattvas Way of Life of Shantideva (Bibliotheca Indo Buddhica Series): Rinpoche, Tharangu (Tr. Ken Holmes & Thomas Doctor).

Religious History of Ladakh (Bibliotheca Indo Buddhica Series): Jina, Prem Singh (Ed.).

The Symbolism of the Stupa by Snodgrass, Adrian.

Buddhism and Ecology by Bachelor, Martine and Brown, Kerry.

The Ancient Egyptian Buddha: The Ancient Egyptian Origins of Buddhism (Hardcover) by Muata Ash.

Buddhism in Medieval Japan (Institute of Buddhist Studies) by James C. Dobbins.

Pali Buddhism (Curzon Studies in Asian Philosophy) by Frank Hoffman.

A Survey of Buddhist Thought by Alfred Scheepers.

Awakening the Buddha Within: Tibetan Wisdom for the Western World by Lama Surya Das.

Introduction to Buddhism: An Explanation of the Buddhist Way of Life by Geshe Kelsang Gyatso.

Elements of Buddhist Iconography by Anand K. Coomaraswamy.

Encyclopaedia of Buddhist Tantra by Shiv Shanker Tiwary. New Delhi.

Ambedkar and Buddhism by Sangharakshita. Delhi, Motilal Banarsidass.

Ancient Buddhist Monasteries: India and Nepal by S. Gajrani. 1998.

Asoka: The Buddhist Emperor of India by Vincent A. Smith. Third Edition.

Asoka by D.R. Bhandarkar. Reprint. New Delhi, AES, 2000.

Asoka the Great by D.C. Ahir. 1995.

The Basic Conception of Buddhism by Vidhushekhara Bhattacharya. Reprint. Delhi, Universal Voice, 2007.

Buddhism: Religion and Meditation by S. Jafar Mahmud. 1998.

Buddhism in India and Sri Lanka: (C. 300 BC to C. 600 AD): A Comparative Study by S.M. Haldhar. New Delhi, OM Publications, 2001.

Buddhism in Indian History and Culture (Upto the Ambedkar Movement) by S.R. Goyal. Jodhpur, Kusumanjali Book World, 2004.

Buddhism in South-East Asia: A Cultural Survey by D.C. Ahir. Delhi, Satguru, 2001.

Buddhist Art and Thought by Shashibala. New Delhi, Akshaya Prakashan, 2007.

Cultural Horizons of India, Volume 5: Studies in Tantra and Buddhism, Art and Archaeology, Language and Literature by Lokesh Chandra. 1997.

A Universal Buddhist Technique of Meditation by D.C. Ahir.

Meditation Now: Inner Peace Through Inner Wisdom by S.N. Goenka.

The Discourse Summaries by S.N. Goenka.

Essence of Tipitaka by U Ko Lay.

A History of Indian Buddhism: From Sakyamuni to Early Mahayana. Honolulu, HI: University of Hawaii Press, 1990.

Bibliography on Indian Buddhist Art and Archaeology by Utpal Chakraborty.

Meeting the Buddha: On Pilgrimage in Buddhist India by Aitken, Molly Emma.

Buddhism: Its Historical, Theoretical and Popular Aspects by Ernest J. Eitel–2009 manuscript.

Jatakas in Buddhist Thought and Art, 2 Vols. By B. Subrahmanyam–2009.

Buddhism in India: A Historical Survey by Kanai Lal Hazra–2008.

The Ashoka (Amar Chitra Katha-Hindi).

Buddhist View of Knowledge and Reality by Moti Lal Pandit–2008.

Samrat Ashok by M.I. Rajaswi.

Index